CYCLE RACING

THIS IS A CARLTON BOOK

This edition published by Carlton Books Limited 2006
20 Mortimer Street
London W1T 3JW

Text copyright © 2004 William Fotheringham
Design copyright © 2004 Carlton Publishing Group

ISBN-10 1-84442-716-1
ISBN-13 978-1-84442-716-1

AUTHOR DETAILS
William Fotheringham writes on cycling and rugby for the *Guardian* and *Observer*, and is the author of *Put me Back on my Bike: In Search of Tom Simpson* and *Fotheringham's Sporting Trivia*.

ACKNOWLEDGEMENTS
For their contributions to the original version of this book, I would again like to thank Doctor Chris Jarvis and Tim Clifford, who supplied much of the material in chapters 13 and 7 respectively, and Dave Smith, for the interval training information, as well as Jim Hendry, Nick Rearden, Anita Bean, Steve Paulding, Ron and Sam Collins, Giles Haley, Jenny Copnall and James Beechinor-Collins. I remain in their debt, and second time around, additional thanks are due to Nicky Crowther, Graeme Freestone-King, John Dowling, Ian Drake, Roger Wilbraham and Keith Flory for their comments, and Gus Ferguson for the cartoons in chapter 11. At Carlton Books, thanks to Roland Hall and Jim Lockwood for their efforts and their patience. My sports editor at the *Guardian*, Ben Clissitt, was unstinting as ever in his support, while Caroline, Patrick and Miranda have shown almost unswerving patience in spite of long absences in front of the Mac or in the saddle.

Executive Editor: Roland Hall
Art Direction: Jim Lockwood
Design: Mitch Davies
Illustrations: Peter Liddiard
Picture Research: Stephen O'Kelly
Production: Lisa French

Printed in Dubai.

The publishers would like to thank the following sources for their kind permission to reproduce the pictures in this book: **Buzz Pictures:** 29, 31, (Geoff Waugh): 13, 79. **Corbis Images:** (Francisco Villaflor): 18. **Empics:** (Boris Roessler): 60. **Getty Images:** (Doug Pensinger): 50-1, (Franck Fife/AFP): 4-5, (Joel Saget/AFP): 6-7, (Paolo Cocco/AFP): 53, 122, 120-1. **Graham Watson:** 10, 14, 16, 35, 37, 39, 48-9, 56-7, 58-9, 62-3, 64-5, 66, 68-9, 72, 74, 75t, 75b, 86, 88t, 88bl, 88br, 93, 94, 96, 97, 98, 99, 100, 103, 106, 107, 108, 109, 113, 114, 116, 128, 136, 137, 138, 140, 141, 145, 146, 148, 150, 151, 152, 153, 154. **Polar:** 9, 32-3, 40-1, 43, 76-7, 80, 90-1, 110-1. **Offside:** 55. **Rocky Mountain:** 44-5. Also, special thanks to: **Assos, Colnago, Campagnolo, Cannondale, Giro, Madison Cycles, Pinarello, Scott, and Shimano.**

This book is a revised and updated edition of *Cycle Racing* published by A & C Black in 1996.

CYCLE RACING
HOW TO TRAIN, RACE AND WIN
○ Road Racing ○ Time Trialling ○ Mountain Bike Racing ○ Track Racing ○ Cyclo-Cross

WILLIAM FOTHERINGHAM

ENDORSED BY

BRITISH CYCLING

CARLTON
BOOKS

CONTENTS

I: **GETTING STARTED**

THE WORLD OF CYCLE SPORT IS RICH AND VARIED, OFFERING A RANGE OF RACING FROM THE TOUR DE FRANCE TO THE LOWLY TIME TRIAL. HERE IS A BEGINNER'S GUIDE TO THE MANY SIDES OF CYCLING, WHERE IT ALL HAPPENS, WHAT YOU NEED AND HOW IT ALL WORKS, PLUS HANDY POINTERS TO HELP YOU FIND A CLUB THAT'S RIGHT FOR YOU.

Cycling is a sport with many faces: the high drama and suffering of the Tour de France; the 40-mile-per-hour thrills and spills of mountain-bike downhilling; the silence, broken only by the swish of tyres, of a British Sunday morning time trial; the mellow comradeship of a midweek track racing league.

The fact that one basic skill — riding a bike — offers the chance to compete in what amount to several different sports, but with the same basic training, is what keeps many people attached to bike racing for the whole of their lives. If you are fit enough, and sufficiently well organized, you can take part in four completely different kinds of bike race over an Easter weekend, for example. Few sports offer such variety.

The other long-term attraction of all sides of bike racing is the fact that the basic training is in itself a social act. The only way to train for cycling is by riding a bike, and the most appropriate way to do that — apart from when you are looking to achieve specific ends in your training — is in company.

You can't sustain a decent conversation out jogging or while training on the rugby pitch, but you can while acquiring or maintaining basic fitness for cycle racing. And it's a great way to see the countryside — although sometimes you may be concentrating too hard to notice much of it.

For the newcomer, with so much to choose from, cycling can be a bewildering sport, and it can also be one into which it is hard to find your way initially.

The first priority of this book, then, is to guide you through the types of cycle sport, and to help you gain some idea of what they can offer to you and how you can get started.

ROAD RACING

WHAT IS IT?

Road racing is the most high-profile side of cycle racing. The basic idea is simplicity itself — a field of cyclists starts together and the first across the finish line wins, for which reason road racing was originally known as "mass start". But road races come in all shapes and sizes.

At the top of the pyramid are the great continental Tours, multi-day races such as the Tour de France, Giro d'Italia and Vuelta a España, run in a series of individual stages around each country with the daily results combined to decide an overall classification. With 21 days' racing and a distance of around 2,000–2,500 miles, including mountain climbs in the Alps and Pyrenees, they are among world sport's hardest endurance events. The Tour de France, most important of the big three, rates as the world's biggest annual sporting event: only the Olympics and football's World Cup eclipse it in scale.

Continental Europe is also the home of the one-day Classics: up to 170 miles in length and indelibly rooted in their own area of Europe, they date from the turn of the century. Professional road racing is based on the calendar of races across Europe between February and October, which are used by the stars to build up to the high points of the year: the three Tours, the Classics, the other World Cup counting events, and the annual world championship road race in October. The European professional calendar is contested by about 50 teams totalling some 1,000 cyclists who effectively rank as the best in the world. The UK has a number of events of lesser scale, topped by a series of one-day events that make up the Premier Calendar, and is almost wholly amateur.

HOW DO I DO IT?

The British road-racing season lasts from February to October, and is at its height in May, June and July. Road races are organized by local cycling clubs and leagues under the rules of the governing body, British Cycling (BC). In addition, a number of "independent" road-racing organizations have sprung up in recent years, organizing events on a local basis, mainly for veterans: these provide a straightforward way into the sport. (See useful addresses on page 11.)

There is a wide variety of events for the beginner, ranging from short races (20 miles to 35 miles) on purpose-built circuits on midweek evenings in major cities, to events between 40 miles and 100 miles in distance, usually on a Sunday, on open roads in the countryside. Organization tends to be low key and relatively informal, but a good standard of fitness and experience of riding in a group is necessary even at the lowest level. Fields in races on open roads, shared with normal traffic, are usually limited to 60 or 80 competitors. Races on purpose-built circuits have no restriction on numbers. At the top end, the 100-mile-plus weekend races in the Premier Calendar series are limited to the country's elite racers.

There is a limited number of veterans or women-only races, the toughest of which are included in the season-long BC veterans' series and the season-long BC women's series; there are also series of events for juniors and under-23s. In addition, women and veterans (over-40) can race in those events for senior amateurs which are open to them. The "independent" races cater mainly for veterans, who race in age categories.

British road racing is based on a category system. Over-18 racers split into

Road racing is the most
complex side of cycling,
but also potentially the
most rewarding

five categories: elite category includes all riders of superior ability up to those competing for Olympic selection, first and second and third category are essentially intermediate, and fourth category is for entry-level riders. Transfer from one category to another is based on points awarded according to finishing position in races, which are graded according to length. Scoring a certain number of points takes you up a category; once you are a second or first category, failure to score a fixed number of points in a year results in "relegation".

Juniors, between the ages of 16 and 18, are allowed to race with third-category amateurs in races up to 60 miles, and also compete in a series of elite races that decide world championship selection.

Juveniles, or under-16s, are allowed to race only on circuits that are not open to normal traffic. Like the other categories, they too have a national points series subdivided into age groups down to 8. BC issue under-12 and under-16 racing licences from £6, and encourage race organizers to offer separate prize lists for the youth categories, and, where possible, separate races. To conserve youthful legs for the future, their events are no longer than an hour.

WHAT DO I NEED?

To compete in most British road races, you need to be a member of BC and hold a BC racing licence, which can be bought direct from them, or through a cycling club affiliated to them. Club membership is to be recommended for the beginner, as the advice other riders can offer is crucial, while at a slightly higher level road racing is a team sport, as will be explained in Chapter 6. Club subscriptions are not usually more than £20–£30.

All three levels of BC membership include a "provisional licence", which you can use to ride entry-level events in most disciplines. To race above entry level, you need membership and a racing licence.

In 2004 the licence and BC membership together cost either £62 (silver) or £88 (gold) for a senior member for a full year, with reduced rates for

Aerodynamic excellence in action: David Millar of Britain races the clock

juniors and juveniles. Gold membership includes full accident insurance, four copies of the BC racing calendar and a regular emailed newsletter. There are more details on the BC website www.britishcycling.org.uk, or via their membership services department on 0161 274 2010.

The website is packed with information, including full racing calendar, rules of racing, club and coaching guide and hints for newcomers to the sport. The racing calendar is currently published in four instalments during the year, with club information and rulebook published in a separate directory, but from 2005 BC may revert to a handbook containing all its information, published annually.

Entry fees for road races are between £10 and £20. Most BC-registered races can be entered three weeks beforehand, using entry forms available from cycling clubs or BC. Many events can also be entered on the day.

BC recommend race organizers run special entry-level events where you can turn up and ride with a four-category licence, a provisional licence or no licence at all. These áre to be recommended if you are dipping your toes in the water. Other than that, you need a standard road-racing bike (see Chapter 2). Hard shell helmets are compulsory.

CONTACTS

British Cycling, National Cycling Centre, Stuart St, Manchester, M11 4DQ. Telephone: **0870 871 2000**.
Website: **www.britishcycling.org.uk**
Governing body for road racing, cyclocross, mountain biking, track racing, BMX, 4-Cross and cycle speedway.

League of Veteran Racing Cyclists
77 Hulme Hall Road, Cheadle Hulme, Cheshire SK8 6JZ.
Telephone: **0161 485 7969**.
Website: **www.lvrc.org/**
Specializes in handicap events for veterans. Not affiliated to BC.

The Surrey League
Website: **www.surreyleague.co.uk**
UK's biggest race organizer, based south of London, specializing in events at grassroots level. Affiliated to BC.

Women's Cycle Racing Association, 34 Orion Way, Braintree, Essex CM7 9UR.
Website: **www.wcra.org.uk**
E-mail: **membership@wcra.org.uk**
Devoted to promoting women's racing. Affiliated to BC.

TIME TRIALLING

WHAT IS IT?
The time trial is cycling stripped to the basics: starting at one- or two-minute intervals, riders race "alone and unassisted" and are timed over a course of a set length; the fastest wins. It's as simple as that: a pure test of speed and strength. "The race of truth" is its European nickname.

Time trialling has two faces. Internationally, there are men and women's world time-trial championships, while the great Tours always include several time-trial stages: as a way of deciding who is the strongest in a multi-day race, the time trial has no equal.

In Britain, time trialling developed from the turn of the century onward as a secret, isolated culture, since racing of any kind on the open road was banned until just before the Second World War. Time trials were run in lonely places at the crack of dawn on Sundays and ridden by racers dressed in black, on courses referred to by code numbers to preserve secrecy.

Nowadays, time trialling is still the most popular form of cycle sport in Britain, even if the only really high-profile events are the national championships at the fixed distances. These are 10, 25, 50 and 100 miles, usually over courses "out and home" on open roads, shared with other traffic, starting and finishing at the same point. Events lasting 12 hours and 24 hours are decided on the distance covered in the set time. At national level, top riders' average speeds for 50 and 100 miles, and 12 hours, are combined to determine the men's British Best All Rounder. The women's contest is decided over 25, 50, and 100 miles.

HOW DO I DO IT?
Time trialling is very accessible, and relatively cheap for the beginner. "Open" time trials are organized at weekends from February to October by individual clubs and area bodies under the rules of

the British governing body, Cycling Time Trials, or CTT. Organization varies, but owes much to the "private and confidential" tradition: some clubs will hire a village hall for riders to change in, many simply set up a tea stall in a convenient lay-by.

Unofficial, "club" time trials are run over 10 and 25 miles, usually weekly in the evenings during the summer, by an individual cycling club for its members, who simply turn up, pay a nominal fee, collect their number and ride. Usually results will count for a season-long league within the club. Such club events are the foundation of most long-established cycling clubs, which usually have club championships at the various distances, and their own "Best All Rounder" contest.

As well as the more popular "out and home" distances, time trials over hilly circuits ranging from 17 to 75 miles are increasingly popular as traffic increases on major roads. There are other variants: time trials are run for teams of two, three or four cyclists, and at the end of the season come the traditional "hill climbs" — short, painful, time trials that simply start at the bottom of a local hill and finish at the top.

Within most "open" time trials, there are separate prize lists for veterans (over-40), women, juniors (under-18) and juveniles (under-16), although these categories have their own events as well, and their own national championships. Some veterans' events are run on an age-based system wherein the riders are competing against each other and against the "standard" time for their age group.

Fields in "open" events are limited to 120, and, for popular races, the field will be selected on qualifying times for the distance. Fortunately for the beginner, acquiring a qualifying time in a club time trial is not difficult.

WHAT DO I NEED?

To ride time trials you simply have to be a member of one of the 900 cycling clubs affiliated to CTT: cycling club subscriptions, between £20 and £30 per year, usually include CTT membership. Entry to "club" events usually costs not more than £1.50. Beginners can "turn up and Tri" a club time trial without membership of anything more than the human race. As you are racing on the open road, you have to be at least 12,

and, for under-18s, parental authorization is necessary.

The Cycling Time Trials website, **http://www.cyclingtimetrials.org.uk/** includes intro-ductions to time trialling for young cyclists and beginners, hints on safety, and details of their calendar, rules and records.

"Open" time trials are listed on the CTT website and in their handbook, which is available from cycling club secretaries and via their website. It also includes a list of all courses registered with the RTTC, which are still referred to by the pre-war system of codes. Entry fees are rarely more than £10, except for some long-distance events. "Open" races have to be entered in advance, on forms available from CTT via their website or club secretaries.

Time trials can be ridden on any kind of bike, but the best to start with is a standard road-racing bike, with a few modifications (see Chapter 2). Helmets are compulsory for under-18s, but are strongly recommended for all age groups.

CONTACTS

Cycling Time Trials, 77 Arlington Drive, Pennington, Leigh, Lancs WN7 3QP.
Telephone: **01942 603976**.
Fax: **01942 262326**.
Website: **www.cyclingtimetrials.org.uk/**
E-mail:
phil.heaton@cyclingtimetrials.org.uk

MOUNTAIN-BIKE RACING

WHAT IS IT?

Mountain-bike racing grew rapidly in the 1990s but has peaked in popularity: its inclusion in the Olympics for the first time in 1996 came less than 20 years since the first weekend racers began zooming down mountain trails in California on adapted "clunkers". Little did they suspect that their quest for speed and fun would give birth to a worldwide off-road sport, and that mountain-bike sales would end up outstripping those of traditional road bikes.

Now, top mountain-bike racers specialize in one of two disciplines. The gruelling "cross-country" is run on road-race lines over two to three hours across hilly, if not necessarily mountainous, terrain; and the spectacular "downhill", is essentially a solo time trial literally down the side of a mountain, which can be

compared to downhill skiing in its demands. Dual-slalom and four-cross are variants of downhill in which two or four racers compete simultaneously; it is expected that four-cross, which is over a shorter course, will grow rapidly in the near future.

The professional mountain-bike racing scene has expanded rapidly to include several hundred top men and women from all around the world, who contest an annual world championships and the World Cup, a season-long, worldwide series of downhill and cross-country races. Early on, Britain was one of the strongest countries in mountain-bike racing, winning several medals at world championships. The competition has recently grown more intense although British downhillers still enjoy considerable success.

Because cross-country is tough and tends only to reward the elite, the trend currently in the UK is away from pure racing towards longer events which marry physical challenge and fun such as 24-hour team races and mass participation events known as "enduros". Downhill racing has, however, grown in popularity in recent years, and there are now series in Scotland, Wales, England and the Midlands as well as a British national series.

HOW DO I DO IT?

Mountain-bike races are extremely accessible, if not cheap, to enter, and the emphasis at all but elite levels is placed firmly on having a good time. Races for mountain bikes now take place all year round in Britain, peaking in summer, and tailing off to two or three races a week in the winter.

Race meetings tend to offer a good range of races across the various categories, meaning that the beginner can usually find his or her competitive level relatively quickly. Categories are decided according to the year of your birth, with the minimum age being 12. The senior category runs from 23–29; other categories are novice men and women, juvenile (12–14), youth (15–16) juniors (17–18), under-23 (19–23) The other classes are masters (30–39), veterans (40–49), and super veterans (over 50).

Courses vary from flat to mountainous, depending on the area of the country in which the race is held.

Steve Peat: mountain bike
racing isn't just about
plugging through the mud

Venues range from London parks to a purpose-built circuit in Sussex, the grounds of country houses, and the Scottish and Welsh mountains.

Who races with whom depends on the scale of the promotion. At the top of the mountain-biking pyramid are the national championships, and the season-long, national cross-country and downhill points series: these typically include separate races for each category. Smaller promotions may combine categories, but should run to separate prize lists. The emphasis is on fun, with trade stalls, pre-race pasta parties and trick riding displays creating a fairground atmosphere at major events, which could not be further removed from the typically low-key time trial.

WHAT DO I NEED?

Entering a mountain-bike event is straightforward. Apart from the National Points series events, where you should enter in advance, you can turn up on the day, pay your money and ride in most events, although enduros and downhills tend to need pre-entry. Entry fees are between £15 and £25 for cross-country, and £20–45 for downhill due to extra costs such as venue hire and "uplift" — getting the riders from bottom to top of the slope. However, the fees often include giveaways such as a free T-shirt, free entry to the pasta party etc. Membership of a mountain-bike club is not necessary.

A single licence issued by BC gives cyclists entry to mountain-bike races run under their rules as well as road and track races; you may not need a licence for many mountain-bike events and should check with the organizer. Many events are listed in BC's racing calendar and on their website as well as specialist magazines such as Mountain Biking UK.

The rules stipulate that you must ride a mountain bike (see Chapter 2), and wear a hard shell helmet.

CONTACTS

British Cycling, National Cycling Centre, Stuart St, Manchester, M11 4DQ.
Telephone: **0870 871 2000**.
Website: **www.britishcycling.org.uk**

Pursuit of perfection: Leontien van Moorsel of Holland tackles the track

TRACK RACING

WHAT IS IT?

Track racing is the most spectator-friendly and spectacular arm of cycle sport, with the action confined to a small (250 metres to one kilometre), oval, banked circuit also known as a velodrome. These can be indoor or outside, with a surface of either concrete or wood planking. The steepness of the banking depends on the size of the track: on a small track, it will be up to 45 degrees.

At its zenith immediately after the Second World War, when tens of thousands of spectators would flock to stadia such as London's Herne Hill and the Velodrome d'Hiver in Paris, track racing has since declined steadily in popularity. Attempts are being made to relaunch the sport internationally, and it is likely that as traffic congestion threatens racing on open roads, track racing will grow again.

Cycling's international governing body recognizes a variety of disciplines on the track at world championships level, and a typical track meeting, sometimes held over several days, will include a variety of events.

The sprint is usually over one kilometre with the fastest man to the finish line the winner. A series of elimination rounds between two or three riders decides the two finalists. The team sprint is a three-man, three-lap timed event with a qualifying round followed by quarter-final, semi-final and final where it is team against team.

The pursuit is over 4 kilometres for men (3 kilometres for women), with two riders starting precisely half a lap apart, and "pursuing" each other for the distance. The aim is to catch the opponent: more often the winner is simply the fastest over the set distance. Again, a series of elimination rounds culminates in a final between the two fastest riders. The team pursuit is run on similar lines, over 4 kilometres, between teams of four riders.

The distance race, usually over 10 or 20 kilometres, is essentially the same as a road race, with 20 or 30 riders starting together and the first man across the finish line the winner. The points race is over a similar distance and format, with the riders sprinting for points every few laps, and the highest scorer winning. The Madison is contested over distances up to 50 kilometres by teams of two riders.

The keirin is a big-money sport in its own right in Japan, and involves a group of half a dozen riders being paced to sprint speed by a moped, then being left to fight it out among themselves for first place. The elimination race, or "Devil-take-the-hindmost", is equally spectacular, with the last rider across the line each lap eliminated until two men are left to sprint it out. Toughest of all, the one-kilometre time trial demands the ability to measure an effort for just over a minute.

HOW DO I DO IT?

Track racing in Britain is growing again with the indoor tracks at Manchester and Newport, Gwent, supplementing the variety of outdoor tracks across the country. A new velodrome for London is proposed as part of the city's 2012 Olympic bid. As well as the Revolution series at Manchester there are other big track meets across the country at stadia such as London's Herne Hill, Welwyn, and Meadowbank, Edinburgh. The Herne Hill meeting on Good Friday is the longest established, but, being outdoors, it is frequently a victim of the British weather!

Track racing in Britain is run under the rules of BC, who also organize the annual national championships, which include a vast number of age categories from under-12 to 70-plus. Several major meetings during the season include rounds of the national season-long series in the various disciplines and age groups.

The foundation of British track racing is the local track league. Typically, these are held on midweek evenings during the summer, with a variety of events each evening all counting towards a season-long championship. Organization is informal, and the atmosphere on a warm summer evening is relaxing — on a chilly night in May, thermals are recommended!

Most track leagues have training sessions for novice riders, which are to be recommended, as riding a banked track is a technique that has to be acquired. There are other attractions for the novice: track leagues tend to stream their fields, so that you won't have to compete immediately against the best riders; in addition, with several events during the evening, you have more than one chance to compete.

Track leagues usually organize separate events for women and under-16s:

juniors may compete with seniors, who race in the same categories as on the road.

WHAT DO I NEED?

The same BC racing licence as that used for road racing and mountain-bike racing also gains you entry to track races. The BC directory and website include a full list of all the track leagues and tracks in the UK.

The track bike is a specialized item (see Chapter 2), but some tracks have their own bikes for hire to beginners who want to have a go at track racing. Hard shell helmets are compulsory.

CONTACTS

British Cycling, National Cycling Centre, Stuart St, Manchester, M11 4DQ.
Telephone: **0870 871 2000**.
Website: **www.britishcycling.org.uk**

Fast and furious: cyclo-cross is road racing's winter relative

CYCLO-CROSS

WHAT IS IT?

Cyclo-cross is a winter form of road racing run on small off-road circuits, usually in a city park, using adapted road-racing bikes. It predates mountain-bike racing by several decades, but is slowly declining in popularity due to the arrival of mountain-bike racing. Races are rarely more than an hour in length, and require running and bike-handling skills as well as pedalling strength.

In Europe, there are a hundred or so professional cyclo-cross men, and the sport is particularly popular in Switzerland and Belgium. There is increasing cross-over with mountain bike racing: many European off-road racers ride cyclo-cross in winter, then turn their attention to the mountain-bike circuit in summer. The annual world championships in February are the high point of the season, and major European cyclo-crosses count towards a winter-long World Cup.

HOW DO I DO IT?

Cyclo-cross races take place all winter in Britain under the rules of British Cycling and are listed in BC's directory and website. Apart from the major events such as the national championships and National Series, they tend to be low-key, informal events run by local cycling clubs, often organized into area leagues

over several weekends.

British cyclo-crosses are increasingly contested by riders on mountain bikes as well as the conventional 'cross machines, and some meetings have separate mountain-bike prize lists, or separate mountain-bike events.

Even at local level, cyclo-cross is not for the fainthearted: the races are short, but challenging. A certain amount of road-racing or mountain-biking experience is to be recommended.

National championships are held for senior men and women, veteran men (over-40), juniors (16–18) and juveniles (under-16s), but local meetings usually consist of one race, normally about an hour, for senior men and women and juniors combined, plus a shorter event for juveniles.

All cyclo-cross meetings include an under-12 event, with free entry, and juvenile events include separate prize lists for under-12s.

WHAT DO I NEED?

At most cyclo-cross races, apart from the major events, you can turn up on the day and enter on the line. A full calendar of races can be found in the BC directory and on the website.

Cyclo-cross rules stipulate that any kind of bike, including mountain bikes, can be used, but the traditional adapted road-racing bike, described in Chapter 2, is recommended if you are going to ride seriously. Helmets are compulsory.

CONTACTS

British Cycling, National Cycling Centre, Stuart St, Manchester, M11 4DQ.
Telephone: **0870 871 2000**.
Website **www.britishcycling.org.uk**

"NON-COMPETITIVE" EVENTS

Many British and American cyclists are increasingly keen to participate in well-organized mass road events over challenging courses; these are not supposed to be competitive but can be harder than any amateur race and, at the front at least, can be as hotly contested. Events such as the Etape du Tour — held annually over a mountain stage of the Tour de France — provide an unmatched two-wheeled experience as well as a physical challenge, and are highly recommended. For British cyclists, the best way to participate can be through a specialist cycling holiday company such as Graham Baxter Sporting Tours (**www.sportingtours.co.uk**).

THE CYCLING CLUB

If you want to ride bike races, you don't have to join a cycling club, but there are a variety of good reasons to do so. The best one is that cycling is in itself a social activity. The miles of training that you need to put in, usually over the winter, to gain basic fitness for whatever type or types of racing you get into, will pass a whole lot quicker if you find like-minded people to share them with.

Most cycling clubs organize group rides or "clubruns" through the winter on Saturdays, Sundays or both; many run informal midweek training sessions through the summer. At the bare minimum, a cycling club will put you in touch with potential training partners. And it is a whole lot easier to go out training when the weather looks doubtful — as at some point it certainly will — if you've already made a date to meet "the lads" or "the girls".

Almost as important is the fact that cycling clubs will be able to help you find your way in racing. Whether it be mountain biking, road racing, track, or whatever, they have secretaries who can get you a BC licence and the handbooks published by BC and Cycling Time Trials. Hopefully, older, more experienced members will be able to advise you on which races to begin with, and will offer tips on technique. The club should have a coach, or should at least be able to put you in touch with one, and he will be able to advise you on your training and diet etc. If they can't or won't help you out, you would be well advised to take your subscription elsewhere.

If you're going to ride time trials — and they are the easiest and most accessible way of assessing your potential on the road — you will find it hard to get by without joining a club affiliated to CTT, which runs its own informal time trials.

For potential road and track racers, the need to join a cycling club is paramount, as only by riding in a group regularly will you acquire the ability to rub shoulders at speed in a group that is basic to road racing and some track disciplines. In road racing you'll find it hard psychologically and physically to compete against clubs who turn up in numbers unless you too have your own "team".

In mountain biking and cyclo-cross, you can be a lone wolf: there's less need for the support a cycling club can give. But big mountain-bike races are the most social form of bike racing — those pasta parties, those endless afternoons spent comparing bouncy forks! — and nothing quite beats the sheer what-the-hell fun of a group mountain-bike ride.

FINDING A CYCLING CLUB

- National governing bodies such as BC and CTT will put you in contact with affiliated clubs in your area. The BC website carries a club directory, including clubs in its Go-Ride programme, and also carries listings for mountain-bike clubs.
- Get several different clubs' contact numbers, then be prepared to shop around. The best club for you may not be the closest to you.
- Specialist bike shops may be able to help you find a local club — if you get into the sport, you're a potential customer for them.
- Centres such as velodromes and purpose-built racing circuits may have lists of local clubs — and you can always turn up at a race and ask around.
- Mountain-bike clubs and contacts are listed in magazines such as *Mountain Biking UK*.
- It sounds daft, but a lot of cyclists find clubs by catching up a racing cyclist on the road and asking them for advice.

QUESTIONS YOU SHOULD ASK A CLUB CONTACT

- What help do they give to beginners? Or are they only interested in established racers?
- How many young riders/women/veterans does the club have? At what level do they race?
- Do they have a coach?
- If you want to ride road or track races, do they have many road or track racers in the club, and what level are they?
- Do they organize clubruns, and road-race training sessions? If so, what levels of ability do they cater for?
- If you want to ride time trials, do they organize club events?

If the answer to any of these questions is no, it's probably worth looking elsewhere, if there are other clubs in your immediate area.

JOINING A CLUB

The process of finding the right cycling club for your needs is worth taking a little time over: if you join one that is inappropriate, you will certainly miss out on a lot of fun, and possibly a lot of useful advice, before you discover the right one. Most reasonable-sized towns have more than one club: often one will specialize in time trialling, another in road and track racing. Phone them all up and try to find out what they do.

The ideal club for the beginner is one with a good pool of riders who want to ride similar races at a similar level, which organizes club time trials and clubruns for riders of all abilities, and which has a coach and/or experienced riders who are willing to hand down advice. If you find one of these, you're there.

Most cycling clubs have a meeting point where they gather on one or two evenings during the week: go down, get more information, and get the feel of the club. Bear in mind that the people in the clubroom may not be the ones you want to meet — many racers who work don't have time to go down to the club every week, while officials such as the club secretary usually have to be there — so if you're out to discover, for example, what the road racers in the club are like, find out where they train and go out and meet them.

Most cycling clubs are basically friendly, but not well geared up to looking after the newcomer: it will take a while to establish yourself on the road. If your first meeting with them is a group ride of any kind, go with the flow. You are meeting a group who have become closely knit through shared suffering over several years, and it may take a little time to gain acceptance. Don't get into mock race situations — you may come up against a rider who delights in making newcomers suffer. If you don't feel welcome after a couple of visits to the clubroom or a couple of group rides, keep shopping around: you will be repaid for your efforts.

GO-RIDE

British Cycling accredits clubs through its nationwide Go-Ride scheme for young cyclists, which is explained in detail on its website www.go-ride.net. These clubs have a coach and essential facilities, offer a wide range of cycling activities for under-18s, and should provide a pathway into BC's structures for aspiring young athletes: they are strongly recommended.

The website includes hints for young cyclists and details of Talent Team, a nationwide on-line competition for young cyclists where you can compare your times and those of your friends. Even more handily, it includes a club-finder section. The process is an ongoing one as clubs join up, so if there is no club listed in your area now, it may be worth looking again in a few months.

2: **EQUIPMENT**

THERE IS A BEWILDERING VARIETY OF BIKES AND BITS ON THE MARKET, SO WHETHER YOU ARE MOUNTAIN BIKING, TIME TRIALLING OR ROAD RACING IT IS VITAL TO WORK OUT YOUR NEEDS BEFORE TAKING THE PLUNGE. WHAT ABOUT YOUR RIDING POSITION? CLOTHING? SHOULD YOU BUY A PULSE MONITOR OR A SET OF BOUNCY FORKS? HERE'S THE LOWDOWN.

You know roughly what you want to do — time trialling, road racing or mountain-bike racing. You've found a club and people to advise you. But then there is another important question to answer. What kind of bike do you need? And what about clothing for racing and training? Suspension forks? A pulse monitor? How important are the sunglasses worth £100?

Two principles are worth bearing in mind. Firstly, don't cut corners. Shoddy equipment will break at vital moments, leaving you a frustrated and possibly bruised person. Good "bits" are available without breaking the bank. If your budget is limited, spend in areas where there is a safety or a performance implication. Aesthetics can come later.

Secondly, try to build up a relationship with a local bike shop; they will be happier to service your machine if you actually buy bits there. If you are nice to them, you may go to the top of the list when you're in a hurry for an emergency repair. Although some of the best-value bikes and bits in the country are available through mail order in magazines, a local bike shop will offer better after-sales service and back-up, so try for a compromise between the two in terms of where you spend your money. And if you are buying a complete bike for the first time, a shop with a good reputation is your best bet: consult local cyclists or the Association of Cycle Traders — the umbrella body for independent retailers in the UK. Their website, **www.act-bicycles.com**, includes recommendations on buying bikes, and a retailer list by UK county. Also worth looking for are bikeshops whose mechanics have the Cytech qualification: **www.cytech-uk.co.uk**.

THE ROAD-RACING BIKE

Whether you race track, time trials or mountain bikes, a road-racing bike will probably be what you spend most of your time on: as you will discover later on, the long, steady distance miles that are the foundation of a cyclist's fitness are best done on the road. To a greater or lesser degree, all racing machines are derived from the road bike, so we will begin by looking at the standard machine then describe its more exotic brethren.

FRAME

This is the heart of the bike. You can't afford to get this wrong. Buy the best you can within your budget. You have a choice of four materials:

Steel and aluminium frames offer the best compromise between longevity, performance and value, but you should not go too far down market. Reynolds 531 remains probably the best-value entry-level steel tubing in use; Deda 01 and Reynolds 653 offer better performance and lower weight. Expect to pay £250–£300 for a hand-made frame made of 531 or equivalent, depending on whether it is "off the peg" or built to measure; 653 will cost a little more.

Aluminium, if built well, can offer a weight and stiffness advantage, particularly for heavier riders, plus it won't rust if you chip the paint. Until recently, steel was best value, but there are now cheap, relatively well-made "off the peg" aluminium frames on the market that are ideal at entry-level. At a slightly higher price and quality bracket Cannondale, Specialized, Trek and Bianchi are among the leading names.

Carbon fibre and titanium can enhance one's performance and reduce weight, but are expensive and outside many people's budgets. For carbon fibre, Trek, Specialized, Cannondale and Bianchi are again names to look for. For titanium it's Merlin and Litespeed.

Make sure the frame fits. The basic guideline is that your frame size should be 66 per cent of your inside leg, but there's far more to it than that. If you are buying for the first time, seek out an ACT-listed (Association of Cycle Traders) bike shop who will measure you properly, and, ideally, let you go for a test ride before selling you something "off the peg". If they are not interested in taking the time to sell you a bike that fits properly, go elsewhere. Comfort and safe handling are paramount — if the bike does not "feel right", ask for advice

If you have very long arms or legs, or, conversely, a short back, you may find that a local specialist frame builder, who can make to measure, serves your purpose better — your local cycling club will know who to recommend. Relatively new to the market are compact frames, offering a slightly shorter down tube and a top tube that slopes upward; these are far more size flexible than standard frames. The leading manufacturer is Giant.

An entire chapter on its own could be written about position on the bike: even riders who have been racing for some time can still benefit from minor adjustments, while if you start riding on a bike with the wrong position, it can take years to get it right. This is why, if you are buying a racing bike for the first time, get help.

WHEELS

After the frame, your wheels are the most important item you will buy. Badly built wheels will fall apart quickly, and offer nothing but trouble, so it is essential to seek out quality.

One increasingly popular option is "complete" wheels, with deep, U-shaped

"aero" rims, made mainly by the specialist wheel company Mavic, and the component makers, Campagnolo and Shimano. These are stiff, aerodynamic and come off the peg, making them the item of choice on most ready-made machines in the upper price brackets. With prices beginning at about £200 for an entry-level model, though, they are not cheap.

If you opt for traditional rims and hubs, find a reputable bike shop to build them up for you, particularly if you are on the heavy side. Hubs made by Campagnolo and Shimano are of a uniformly high standard: you buy longevity and finish according to how much you pay. Even their budget groupsets are good value at entry level. Quick release fixing is vital, and is standard on all quality hubs.

The modern road racing bike: 10 gears, deep-rimmed wheels, and lightweight "clincher" tyres

More important is choice of rim and the number of spokes. The standard choice for road racing is 36 spokes per wheel, which gives a stronger, more flexible wheel, or 32 if you are a lightweight racer. Wheels with 28 spokes

SADDLE ERGONOMICS: HOW TO SIT ON THE BIKE CORRECTLY

(1) With the leg fully extended as you sit on the saddle, your heel should sit on the pedal at its lowest point without the hip rocking. Wear your normal riding shoes when you try this. At the correct saddle height you should easily be able to reach the pedal with the heel when the leg is stretched, and your leg should not quite be extended when the foot is in the pedal at its lowest point.

(2) With the pedals at the "quarter to three" position, your forward knee should be directly above the pedal axle. It's not going too far to employ a plumb line to check this.

(3) With hands on the "drops", and cranks at the "ten to four" position (parallel with the down tube), there should be about 5mm between the elbow and knee.

These customized wheels by Colnago of Italy feature carbon-fibre hubs, deep alloy rims and cut-out quick-release levers

GEARS

Essentially, you have a choice between two manufacturers, Campagnolo and Shimano, and between two changing systems — the old-fashioned, simple levers on the down tube of the frame, which are barely seen now, and more complicated changers incorporated into the brake levers. Campagnolo's system is known as Ergopower, Shimano's as STI.

Both systems "index" the gears: a ratchet system in the levers means that each "click" as you move the levers moves the rear gear mechanism into a pre-set sprocket, giving precise changing. However, the two manufacturers' systems are not compatible, unless you are a skilled mechanic.

For road racing, brake-lever changers are invaluable, simply because you do not have to take your hands off the bars to change gear as was the case with "down-tube" shifters. Thus, you can maintain a good pedalling rate on climbs without having constantly to sit down, change, then stand up again. It means that you can change gear and brake almost at the same time, and that you can change gear at times when both hands must be on the bars, for example when cornering.

Anything that makes life that much easier whether you are road racing or merely training in the hills is to be recommended and Campagnolo's Veloce and Shimano's 105 gearsets are well up to the rigours of road racing. However,

are kept for lighter riders, or for very special road races.

For rims, the prerequisites are strength and lightness, which means aluminium. More expensive rims tend to be heat-treated and anodized for further strength. The best manufacturers are Mavic and Campagnolo.

Don't race on wheels that are out of true or have any loose spokes. Get wheels tightened at the first hint of trouble. The time to check them is immediately after a race, so that you have all week to get them trued before the next race. After a year or so, check the rims periodically for signs of cracking around the spoke holes.

TYRES

For road riding, you have two choices: "high pressures", otherwise known as "clinchers", have a separate casing and inner tube and are held on the rim by stiff beading; tubulars, or "tubs", have integral casing and inner tube and are glued or taped on to the rim.

In performance terms, there is little to choose between them — professional teams use both kinds, but seem to feel that the tubular has a slight edge in "feel". For value and convenience, however, the "clincher" has it every time, as, unlike a tubular, the inner tube can be easily

repaired after a puncture, and there is no messy glue or sticky tape to worry about. For training, entry-level road racing and time trialling, there's no argument: clinchers have it all the way.

Good tyres are as important as a good frame and wheels. Look for the highest-performance "clinchers" on the market, made by firms such as Michelin, Continental and Vittoria. You have a choice of several sizes — 19, 20, 23 and 25 millimetres. Obviously, the narrower the tyre, the lighter it is, but there is a trade-off in comfort, as a slightly wider tyre will flex a little more. At £15–£30 for several months' use, they are excellent value.

If you opt for tubulars, Vittoria's Corsa CX is the standard professional choice, but at £35 a time they are not cheap. They must be stuck on hard — "tubs" have been known to roll off the rim in a race. Don't do this the night before you race: do it several days beforehand and go out for a short ride to "bed in" the tubulars.

Check your tyres carefully after every race — if there are cuts or excessive wear, fit a new one or pair. A blowout could be fatal — literally — so do not skimp in this area. You should always have a spare new tyre in the toolbox, just in case, and two or three new inner tubes.

Campagnolo's Record shifter: sleek and smooth

should be cleaned regularly to reduce wear, and when the sprockets or chain become worn and the chain "jumps" you should replace both at the same time. New sprockets with an old chain, and vice versa, are marriages made in hell.

SADDLE

Most saddles on the market have a plastic base with foam or gel padding, rather than the old-fashioned leather. All sorts of exotic weight-saving materials are on offer, but this should not blind you to the fact that in this area one thing matters: comfort, which is lacking in some extra-light, extra-narrow saddles. So get something adequately padded, and ignore the extra ounce.

Gel padding is good, as the gel is intended to mould itself to the form of your backside, giving extra comfort. Women should look for saddles specially made for wider pelvic bones. Reputable makes include Vetta, San Marco and Selle Italia. Prices should start at around £25.

One final note: for your posterior comfort, the saddle should not point up or down. Put the bike on a level surface and check with a spirit level.

PEDALS

In the last decade, pedals with quick-release bindings, where you "click" your foot in and out as you would with a ski binding, have taken over the market. LOOK, Time and Shimano are the three main types on the market, all with different types of fitting, which are compatible only with the maker's own shoe-plate. At entry level, expect to pay around £40 upwards.

The position of the plate that clicks into the pedal is vitally important — if it is wrong, you can damage your knees. The axle of the pedal should be below the ball of the foot, with the plate in the centre of the sole of the shoe. Initially at least, select pedals that allow a certain amount of

indexed systems require careful adjustment. Check they work perfectly after each race, with the chain dropping precisely into every gear — if your gears slip persistently as you race, you will find yourself in big trouble.

The choice of ratios for road racing is almost standard: both Campagnolo and Shimano offer 18 or 20-speed set-ups with nine or 10 sprockets at the rear and two chainwheels at the front. The standard choice on off-the-peg upmarket road bikes is 53- and 39-tooth chainrings at the front, with a 12–23 toothed cassette at the rear. You may want to ask the shop to fit a 26-tooth sprocket if you live in a hilly area. Schoolboys and juniors should avoid overuse of high gear ratios — they can damage developing muscles. For road racing in these categories, gear ratios are restricted, and the gear size checked before every race.

Indexed gears rely on having the gear cables at the correct tension. As they stretch initially with use, you should check the tension after the first few weeks. Chain, sprockets and derailleur cogs

movement, rather than holding the feet rigidly in place. If you are buying clipless pedals for the first time, make sure you follow these rules:

- Ask specifically for a pedal that allows the front of the foot to rotate slightly.
- Ask the shop to fit the special shoe-plate to your shoes. It's worth paying for the job to be done properly.
- If they don't understand the first question, and are unable to carry out the second task, go and find a shop where they can do both these things.

BRAKES

The faster you can slow down, the faster you can ride towards a corner or down a descent. Again, Campagnolo or Shimano are the ones to look for — respectively their Veloce and 105 brakes are adequate for road racing, but you may well want to upgrade if you can afford it.

It's important to change cables and blocks before they wear out, rather than when they wear out, so keep a close eye on them. When the brakes are positioned on the bike, the whole surface of the blocks should meet the rims as you brake, and there should be no back and forward play in the stirrups. If you are road racing or time trialling, make sure that the brakes are set up so that you can undo the quick release if the wheel buckles and starts rubbing the blocks.

There should be no movement where the levers join the handlebars, and the levers should be positioned so that you can ride comfortably with your hands resting on them, arms and wrists slightly bent. Short-reach models are available for those with small hands.

CRANKSET

Here, too, the choice is essentially between Campagnolo and Shimano, and it doesn't make a lot of difference in performance terms. Basically, the more you pay, the longer it should last — a useful consideration if you're big and strong and likely to cause aluminium to fatigue sooner rather than later.

The standard crank length is 170 millimetres. Riders with short legs, or

HANDLEBAR WIDTH: GETTING IT RIGHT

Too Wide   Proper Width   Too Narrow

The arms should not be spread out, nor the chest constricted.

THE TIME-TRIAL BIKE

At entry level, the principal difference to a standard road-racing machine (see page 20) is the addition of triathlon handlebar extensions, or "tri-bars", which enable the rider to adopt a lower, more stretched-out and thus more aerodynamic position. For more details on fitting, see Chapter 5 on time trialling. Basic tri-bars that clip under the handlebars of a road bike cost around £40. At entry level this is the only adaptation that needs to be made to a basic road-racing bike.

Various kinds of aerodynamic wheels are on the market. Spokeless carbon-fibre "disc" wheels give an aerodynamic advantage in still weather, but make handling difficult when the wind is blowing from the side. They have largely been superseded by "tri-spoke" wheels, built with three wide, flat, aerodynamic spokes, which penetrate the air almost as well as a "disc" but allow the air to pass through from the side, and deep-rimmed 16- or 20-spoked wheels such as the Campagnolo Euro and Mavic Ksyrium, which offer similar benefits to a "tri-spoke". From around £250 to £450 a pair they do not come cheap.

who like to pedal quickly, could opt for 165 millimetres, while taller riders can go up a size to 172.5 millimetres. Sizes over 175mm are best left to seasoned riders with long legs.

HANDLEBARS

For road racing, your comfort is the priority. Make sure your bars are aluminium (steel is too heavy) and are made by a reputable manufacturer such as Deda, 3TTT or ITM. The main variable, however, is the width, which will have a major bearing on comfort and performance. The standard size is 40cm, so if you are broad-shouldered move up to 42cm or 44cm bars, and if you are slight down to 38 cm.

The bars should not point downward. When you sit in the saddle with your hands "on the drops", your wrists should be straight. A position with the bars pointing slightly upward should achieve this.

Time trial elegance by Pinarello: smoothed out carbon frame and forks, rear disc wheel and "aero" front

Aero detail: gear shifters on the end of the "tri-bars", with the cables running internally

More sophisticated, and more expensive, aids to speed come in the shape of low-profile frames, in which a smaller front wheel is used to enable the front end to be lowered so that the rider's back is flattened.

This means that the frame can be reduced in size with a long seat tube making up for the lack of height. A set of upturned "cow-horn" handlebars — or a special set of flattened handlebars as in the picture above — may be used in conjunction with the tri-bars.

THE MOUNTAIN BIKE

Expect to spend a minimum of £300 on an entry-level mountain bike strong enough to be raced off-road: look for models from manufacturers such as Trek, Cannondale, Marin, Specialized and Kona. Steel frames are rarely seen now in entry-level machines, where oversized aluminium has almost completely taken over.

Buying the right sized mountain bike is essential. A key difference is that mountain bikes are always sized 2—4 inches smaller than road bikes. On the road the essence of good fit is comfort in the saddle — quite simply that's where road riders spend most of their time. But "comfort in the saddle" is only part of the off-road story.

In both cases, the basic criterion for a correct fit is the same. When in the saddle, the pelvis and hips should remain steady and at the bottom of each pedal stroke the knees should remain slightly bent. To achieve this with a smaller frame size, mountain bikes simply have longer seatposts.

More time is spent out of the saddle off-road, hence the need for a smaller frame size. When you are connected to the bike just by the bars and pedals, weight distribution assumes much greater importance. Watch a group of experienced riders and you will quickly realize that, whether riding uphill, downhill or simply on rough, obstacle-strewn terrain, they spend a lot of time out of the saddle. This enables them to shift their bodyweight around to maintain maximum control over the bike and also to set themselves up with the best line for tackling what lies ahead.

Standing on the pedals also allows riders' arms and legs to act as shock absorbers, damping out vibrations from bumpy trails. A comfortable position should help to do this without overstraining the rider. With the correct combination of top tube and stem length a rider's back should be straight, and leaning forward at about 45 degrees from the horizontal when riding in the saddle with arms that are slightly bent.

The mountain bike front end: cow-horn bars, "ahead" stem clipping straight to the forks, heavy-duty welding and combined brake-gear levers

Rear-suspended mountain bike with disc brakes and Rockshox up front: a classic combination

Handlebars and stem are usually set a couple of inches lower than the saddle, a position that gives improved climbing power. Comfort and control are the most important factors in choosing bar width. Bars need to be slightly wider than your shoulders, and bar-ends offering a variety of positions for the hands are recommended.

The componentry is relatively simple really: indexed gears with the changers combined with the brake levers, or the simple Grip-shift changer, which is incorporated into the hand grips on the bars. Shimano, Sun Tour and SRAM are the main makers. Ratios are lower and wider than on the road — typically a triple chainring at the front with 26, 36, and 46 teeth, and an eight- or nine-speed cassette at the rear with 12—28 teeth.

Double-sided clipless pedals are the almost universal choice now — as with road pedals, the different types are not compatible. Mountain-bike pedals such as Shimano's SPD are also excellent for commuting and training if fitted to a road bike. In fact, they are better, because they can be combined with a mountain-bike shoe which has a recess in the sole for the plate, making walking easier. For initial fitting the same rules apply as for road shoes.

As for the saddle, make sure it is well padded — one of the models with gel to fit your behind can be a good idea.

Starting at less than £200, hydraulic front suspension forks are a must for shock absorption and handling. Reputable manufacturers include Pace, Manitou, Marzocchi and RockShox. If you are buying a mountain bike from the bottom end of the range, and it includes suspension forks, check the maker — cheap and nasty forks are dangerous if ridden seriously off-road.

Rear suspension is standard on custom downhill machines and is becoming cheaper and more fashionable for off-the-peg cross-country bikes. However, "hardtail", as bikes with only front suspension are known, remains the favourite choice for cross-country racing due to its lighter weight.

Good brakes are vital — for your safety and also to enable you to descend with greater confidence. V-brakes are standard mountain-bike issue due to the increased clearance they offer for tyres covered in mud. Hydraulic brakes are an alternative, offering better stopping and lower maintenance, but cost rather more, while hydraulic disc brakes are almost universal in downhill and are being made sufficiently light for use in cross-country racing.

Wheels with 32 spokes are standard because of the reduced weight they offer, and they will need more looking after due to the hammering they will receive. Sealed hubs are a plus point, because you will inevitably race in mud and water.

Tyre choice depends on what kind of surface you will be riding — clay, hardpack, chalk, rocky or sandy soil. Your local bike shop should be able to advise on the best tyre combinations for local conditions. It's worth considering a pair of

Rocky Mountain's rear-damped set up looks chunky but can compete with "hard-tails"

smooth road tyres as well, so that if things get too muddy off-road you can get a work-out on tarmac. Look out for tyres from Specialized, Ritchey, Michelin, and Continental.

THE TRACK BIKE

At its most basic level, the track bike is essentially a road machine stripped of all the extras: a single fixed gear replaces the 16-speed freewheel, and, because the fixed wheel enables the rider to decelerate by "slowing down" the pedals as they rotate, brakes are unnecessary.

Most track events are short, so the frame may be built with less comfortable but more responsive angles than its road equivalent. Whereas the ends of the forks at the rear of a road machine are slotted forward to enable hubs fitted with a quick release to be slipped in and out, those on a track frame will point backward, so that the fixed wheel hub cannot move.

Tyres are lighter than for the road, but wheels are built more strongly to resist the G-forces on banked tracks — in some cases the spokes will be tied together with wire and then soldered where they cross, so that the wheel will not flex.

A basic track machine is relatively cheap at about £500–700, owing to the lack of "extras" — but the sophisticated monocoque carbon-fibre machines used for top-class timed events such as the kilometre can cost ten times that. If you're lucky, your local track may have basic machines of its own that it will hire out for a nominal sum to beginners. Then look around for something second-hand — the local track, or the back pages of cycling magazines are the places to look.

THE CYCLO-CROSS BIKE

Like the basic track bike, the cyclo-cross machine is a version of the standard road machine, but in this case modified for abuse in the mud and gloop of off-road racing in winter. Whereas a mountain bike is designed to be ridden over or down anything, a 'cross bike is intended to be carried through thick mud and up steep climbs, while offering just enough strength and give to be raced off-road.

Sparse and speedy: the classic track bike has a single fixed gear, no brakes and sturdy frame with rear-pointing drop-outs

This innovative cyclo-cross bike combines road gear shifters, mountain bike disc brakes and classic "knobbly" tyres

The result is an intriguing hybrid.

The frame, usually steel or aluminium, has a slightly higher bottom bracket than a standard road frame, so that the pedals won't clip obstacles on the ground, with perhaps slightly longer forks to absorb shock off-road and wider clearances at the forks and bottom bracket to prevent mud building up.

Handlebar gear shifters are standard: there are special indexed levers that fit into the ends of the bars, but Campagnolo and Shimano road shifters are increasingly used. Mountain-bike pedals are more and more popular, while the cantilever brakes popular on mountain bikes in the 1990s were born on the 'cross machine.

Tyres are fatter than for the road, with knobbly grips like those on mountain bike tyres — both tubulars and high-pressure tyres are made specially for cyclo-cross. And the gear ratios will be lower than on the road, typically 40- and 48-tooth chainrings at the front, with a 13–23-tooth freewheel at the back. At the bottom end of what is available, expect to pay about £750. Bear in mind that "off-the-peg" options tend not to be available — most crossmen buy their first bike second-hand.

While the cyclo-cross machine is a specialized animal, it's often forgotten that you can use it for more than cyclo-cross: with the addition of mudguards and the tyres swapped for road models, it can be quickly turned into a winter training or commuting machine.

BEGINNER'S GUIDE TO CLOTHING

JERSEY

Wool has been superseded by a variety of synthetic materials. Look for a size that is not so loose that it flaps in the wind, but not so tight that it restricts your breathing, and be certain that it will cover your lower back when you are leaning forward on the bike.

For racing in cold weather, a long-sleeved jersey is best, or you can wear a short-sleeved jersey with Lycra armwarmers, which can be pulled off if the weather warms up. For hot weather, a jersey with a full-length front zip is nice, as it can be fully opened as you go uphill. Or you can imitate the Tour de France pros and cut the sleeves off.

Always wear something under the jersey — when you crash on- or off-road, the jersey and undervest will slide over

each other, so that you lose less skin. Winter and summer alike, choose a thermal vest that will wick sweat away from the skin and prevent you from freezing when you go downhill. Cotton T-shirts are not recommended, as they retain moisture.

SHORTS

Here, Lycra has succeeded wool, and a good thing too. For your comfort and hygiene, don't wear anything underneath them. They should be close-fitting, and should cover your lower back — choose either "bib shorts", which have integral Lycra braces, or wear braces with normal shorts. The insert in the crutch that cushions your nether regions is more likely now to be made of a synthetic fibre than the old chamois leather — in any case, it should be well padded, and large enough that you don't rub the inside of your thighs on the saddle. As outlined in Chapter 13, buy at least two pairs, and wash each time after use.

SHOES

As important for your comfort as your shorts — or even more so, as you can irreparably damage tendons if they are wrong. You cannot afford to skimp in this area. Expect to pay around £40 for a good pair of entry-level shoes. For time trialling, road and track racing, and training on the road, the soles must be stiff, so that all the power coming from your legs is transmitted to the pedals. If you're using clipless pedals, as you probably will be, laces alone will be uncomfortable — make sure your shoes have several Velcro straps or a ratchet mechanism. They should fit well, but must not be too tight, as your feet will swell in hot weather. Reputable makers include Shimano, Sidi, Carnac, Gaerne, Specialized, Northwave and Time. If you are buying clipless pedals, buy shoes at the same time, and make sure they are perfectly compatible with the plates for the pedals.

For mountain-bike racing, shoes have to be a compromise between stiffness for pedalling using off-road clipless pedals, and suppleness for when you have to get off and walk. The same rule applies as for the road — comfort first.

TRACK MITTS
These Lycra-backed, usually leather-palmed gloves are important for the racer, as they will protect the delicate palms of the hands if you crash and will cushion your hands from road shock as you ride.

GLASSES
This does not necessarily mean sunglasses, as protecting your eyes is as important in the rain as in the sun. Glasses with interchangeable lenses for rain, dull weather and sun are a good idea, particularly for road- and mountain-bike racing, when bits tend to fly in your eyes. Oakley are the best on the market but are expensive; Vetta, Bolle and Briko are also good, and are cheaper.

WINTER KIT
In Britain, much of your long, steady training will be done between December and March, in weather ranging from idyllic to apocalyptic — mostly the latter, in spite of global warming. This means that winter clothing is a key investment.

"Thermal" training tops, leg-warmers

and tights are an obvious must: they are made of tight-fitting Lycra mixes with an insulated lining and often a protective layer in the front to keep the cold out. Tops should stretch down the lower back and, ideally, up the neck. They should be worn with one or two Lifa type vests, which will wick moisture away from the body.

Gore-Tex-fronted fleece or anorak-type tops are costly, but a worthwhile investment for the extra comfort in the cold — just make sure they are tight-fitting. They are not cheap, but make riding in freezing temperatures less unpleasant, and can be used for other outdoor activities such as hill-walking or cross-country skiing.

It's crucial to keep the extremities covered, so buy gloves and covers for your shoes in the same thermal material — or there are Neoprene ones on the market, which warm up with your body heat when they get wet. And don't ignore the head

and ears: some sort of headband or warm hat is essential.

A "racing cape" — a tight-fitting, light rain jacket, specially cut to cover the lower back — is equally important, not just for when it rains, but also as an extra windproof layer if you have to stop in the cold for a puncture. It's also worth carrying one if you are racing in spring and the weather looks uncertain. The best and most expensive ones come in Gore-Tex and are fashion items in themselves.

HELMETS
Compulsory for all racing except time trialling in Britain, hard-shell helmets made of impact-absorbent polystyrene, usually with a plastic "shell" to hold the protective layer together on impact, are now the norm while training and comm-uting for safety-conscious cyclists.

Invest carefully here, as if you race you will be spending a lot of hours in your "shell". Check the fit with the strap done up — it shouldn't be too tight, or too loose. As

Viatcheslav Ekimov in winter rig: gloves, leg-warmers, arm-warmers, overshoes and ear protectors

you go up the price range, you will find that helmets are lighter and better ventilated, and thus more comfortable. You should expect to pay a minimum of around £25. Get a shop to advise you on fit, and look out for makes such as Giro, Vetta, Bell and Specialized.

Make certain, whatever else you do, that your helmet meets at least one of the following test standards: ANSI, Snell Memorial Foundation, or the BSI. Further helmet advice is included in Chapter 13.

TRAINING AIDS

MUDGUARDS

The English winter factor again: training in foul weather is made far more tolerable for you — and, as importantly, for those you train with — if you stop water and mud spraying everywhere. If you have a training machine, keep them on it all year round; if you are training and racing on the same bike, at least put them on at the end of the season.

Super-narrow "racing"-type aluminium mudguards will do little more than look interesting, but are better than nothing if you can't fit anything else on a frame with close clearances. Plastic guards that come partway down the side of the tyre are the standard choice for most racers: they are light, flexible and cheap to replace if they get damaged.

Custom-built or off-the-peg training frames have special "eyes" brazed on to the forks to hold the support for the guards; most off-the-peg racing frames won't have them. If you're buying one frame for both purposes, don't despair. Make sure there is enough clearance around the brake area to accommodate a mudguard, and then you can buy special adaptors to fit in the ends of the forks — nearly all bike shops will sell them.

PULSE MONITOR

This is the most important training aid you can buy. The pulse monitor gives you a fairly objective measurement of how hard you are going, compared to your maximum pulse, and how hard you've been going during the course of a race or training ride.

A cheap and nasty pulse monitor is

utterly frustrating. First it will tell you that your pulse is at resting rate, and a second later that it's at a level where you ought to be having a heart attack. Bear in mind that it's also possible to have too much sophistication: what you need is a monitor from a reputable manufacturer that is accurate. It will be easier to monitor your training if you buy a monitor that permits you to pre-enter the pulse rate area in which you want to train — between 140 and 160 beats per minute, for example (see Chapter 4).

Check the length of the training period the pulse monitor will record. You'll be doing long sessions at low and medium intensity (see Chapter 4), so it needs to store several hours' worth of information. A pulse monitor that will interface with a computer is nice, but probably going a bit far to begin with.

Polar, Vetta and Cateye are reliable names: Polars have the highest reputation, and can usually be mounted on the 'bars, or on the wrist. When you buy one, make sure it comes with a foam sleeve for mounting on the handlebars.

CYCLE COMPUTER

A computer will tell you how far you've been and how fast you are going. Vetta and Cateye are the best-known makes of cycle computer. The most important information for you is distance and time, particularly if you are going to ride time trials. Average speed is convenient to have as a measure of how fast your improvement rate is.

BEGINNER'S TOOLKIT

No matter how friendly your relationship with the local bike shop, you will have to do basic repairs and servicing yourself. So what should your basic toolkit contain, to keep you from taking the smallest problem down to the bike shop?

- A full Allen-key set, as just about everything on a modern bike is adjusted with an Allen key of some kind.
- At least one spare tyre, several spare inner tubes and a puncture repair kit. Spare rim base tape if you're on high pressures. Tubular cement or spare tub tape if you're on tubulars.
- A long pedal spanner. You can use an Allen key, but you won't get the leverage.
- A spoke key, for truing wheels in an emergency. Unless you've learned to build wheels, take them to someone who knows how to correct them when they go out of true or when you break a spoke.
- A chain breaker and a locknut for whatever cassette hub system you have.
- Cable cutters to avoid frayed ends. Some pliers for holding on to cables. Beg some spoke nipples at the bike shop to clip on to the ends of cables.
- Basic chain-cleaning kit, plus degreaser to clean really grubby cogs — and yourself. Chain lubricant.
- Spare brake and gear cables. A small tube of grease for protecting cables.
- Headset, bottom bracket and hub tools as optional extras.

You may well have noticed that this guide has hitherto failed to mention bottom brackets and headsets in any detail. That's because they are bits that are designed to be maintenance free until they wear out, when you get another one put in. Hubs come into the same category for all bar the dedicated amateur mechanic.

The post-race wash is an important routine operation for all professional teams

LOVE YOUR BIKE

Whatever type of bike you have, it's important to remember that, unlike a car, the bike itself will not make you go fast: you are the engine. Posh bikes can be works of art in their own right, but compared to a good-quality, basic, entry-level racing machine they will not enhance performance by more than a few per cent. With a basic racer, which fits properly and has decent wheels and tyres, if you have the will, you can beat the world. The rider counts for far more than the bike.

There are more important things to worry about than whether you own a £3,000 carbon-titanium jewel. If you maintain the bike properly and look it over frequently, changing items such as cables, tyres and transmission before they wear out, you will have few mechanical problems in races. And if you clean the machine regularly, immediately after each race, you will spot potential problems — items wearing out, bits that have worked loose — as you do so.

FURTHER INFORMATION

For reasons of space, this chapter is no more than a basic guide to the racing bike. To become an expert, sign up for a bike mechanics course such as those offered by the Park Tool School (**www.promech.co.uk**). If you are going to spend a lot of time on your bike, one of the books listed below should find its way to your bookshelf very soon indeed: you will save much time, money and heartache.

- *Bicycle Mechanics* — **Ken Evans** and **Steve Snowling**. Out of date and out of print but still the best book on mechanics ever written. Still available from specialist outlets.
- *Zinn and the Art of Mountain Bike Maintenance* — **Lennard Zinn**, Velo Press 2001.
- *Zinn and the Art of Road Bike Maintenance* — **Lennard Zinn**, Velo Press 2000.

- *Bicycling Magazine's Complete Book of Bicycle Maintenance and Repair*, **Jim Langley**, Rodale Books 1999.
- *Mountain Bike Maintenance* — **Mel Allwood**, Carlton Books 2004.

3: TRAINING PRINCIPLES

YOU HAVE YOUR AIMS IN ONE BRANCH OF CYCLING, OR IN SEVERAL, YOU HAVE A BIKE, AND YOU HAVE ENTHUSIASM TO BURN. SO HOW DO YOU GO ABOUT GETTING FIT FOR RACING? WHERE DO YOU FIND A COACH? SHOULD YOU KEEP A TRAINING DIARY? WHAT IS YOUR INTENSITY THRESHOLD? HERE'S A BRIEF GUIDE TO SET YOU ON YOUR WAY.

PROGRAMME YOURSELF

You know that you want to ride road races, mountain-bike races, track or time trials — or perhaps dabble in them all. You have the right kind of bike, and you are basically fit. It's time to start preparing body and mind for competition.

The competitive urge and a bike are not enough. You should have a clear idea of where you are going and how you are going to get there. You need an objective, or objectives, from which you can draw up a plan of action.

Objectives give your cycling a sense of long-term purpose — they are the source of your motivation to train and to construct a training plan. If you have no idea of quite why you should brave the rain, the pain or the lure of fun, you are more likely to stay at home, slip off and take a short cut, or spend Saturday night drinking rather than resting.

Having a purpose makes the whole process of cycling more rewarding. If you simply bash away with no idea of quite why you are spending all this time, energy and money, you may well achieve some good results, but they will bring less satisfaction. You won't be able to say to yourself: "This is what I set out to do and I have done it."

Objectives should not be too vague or too ambitious. When you sit down to work out what you want to achieve — ideally with your club coach or an experienced fellow bike rider who knows your abilities well enough to advise you — you have to be honest with yourself, recognizing your abilities, weaknesses and the time you have available. And you must plan to go ahead step by step.

For example, if you are a road-racing novice, planning to become a first category in one season, or to ride the Tour de France in three years, is likely to lead to disillusionment. It's better to aim first to finish several races in the bunch, then to get a certain number of points on your licence — say 10 for a first season — then to move up to finishing tougher races. Objectives can always be revised upward — and hopefully yours will be.

One of the enduring attractions of time trialling is the fact that objectives are relatively straightforward to set, because you will always achieve a time for a race. Thus you can always aim simply to better your previous best time or to beat a certain time target. Getting "under the hour" for 25 miles is still a key initial target for most time triallists of medium ability, for example.

Try to be specific as well as honest with yourself. Saying that you will aim to beat John Smith has one flaw — on a given day he may puncture or just be off form, which will make your target meaningless. Aiming, say, to beat the hour, to make the first 10 in at least two sports-class mountain-bike races, or to win a "B" class points race at the local track league means you will see your own performances in relation to your target rather than worrying about where John Smith is and what he is doing.

You can have more than one objective in more than one branch of the sport, but you should bear in mind that the more you aim to do, the less time you will have to achieve each goal. Also, bear in mind future and present commitments — such as exams, or moving house.

After a certain amount of experimentation to find your level, you should try to work out what level of competition you would like to arrive at in three or four years, obviously depending on what changes are likely to take place in your personal life. From this, try to set yourself medium- and long-term goals.

Having a game plan for the next few years will mean that you can set targets for a single season of racing, and then subdivide that into four- to eight-week training phases. Thus, each time you train or race you will have an idea of what you want to achieve and where it is leading you in terms of your medium- and long-term goals.

You may find that you have to reappraise your goals: hopefully it will be upward as you progress more quickly than you have expected, but it may be downward if you realize you are aiming too high or that you have other commitments in your life. In this situation, having a coach is of key importance: discuss with him or her the reasons why things have not gone to plan (not "why you have failed") and try to make it into a positive learning experience. There may be factors that are outside your control, for example work commitments or changes in your personal life. Be realistic and honest, set a new goal and go for it!

THE COACH

To set yourself targets and plan your training you will need advice and support. There are talented individuals who can make their own way, with everything falling into place, but most of us are not among their number. A coach — or, less formally, a senior rider who will provide advice — is as important for anyone entering cycling at beginner level as it is for a seasoned international competitor.

What a coach does varies, but it should include advice on training, on diet, on adapting racing to your lifestyle and on racing technique, and this should be based on what you tell the coach about your training, your commitments and

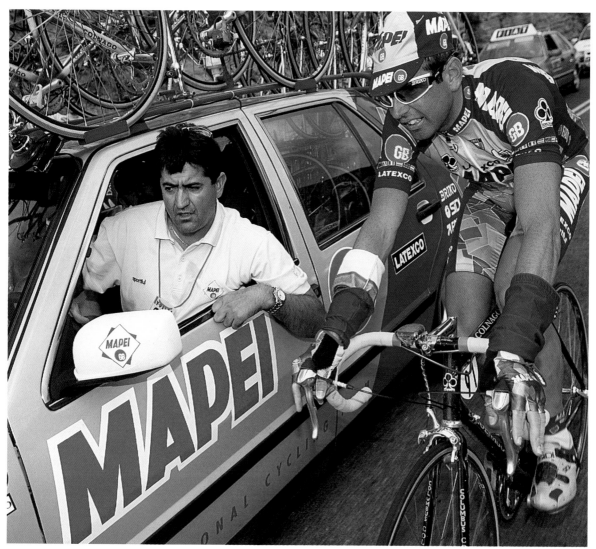

Not everyone can call on a coach in a team car, but it's a vital relationship, even at amateur level

your goals. If you begin working with a coach after having trained yourself for a while, you may well find that having a coach means you actually do less training, but that the training you do is more focused. Most athletes end up overtraining through a fear of undertraining; a coach will probably rein in your enthusiasm and ensure it is properly directed.

If you join a club with a well-established, involved coach, you should not have to look far for advice. The presence of a coach or access to a coaching network should be a key factor in your choice of club. If that is not available, contact British Cycling (BC) or consult their information.

Coaches also exist outside the BC system. Once you have joined a club and feel confident, ask around: find out who the local riders go to for advice and check

them out for yourself.

It may not be as simple as that. If no one presents him- or herself as the coach you need, when you are in doubt about something you will have to look for advice among any experienced and friendly riders you have come across. You will find a plethora of information coming your way, some of it contradictory, for there are different theories on most elements of cycling.

Don't act on it all: sift it according to common sense, try it out, remember who gave you advice that worked and who seemed most interested in helping you out, and eventually you will work out who will be the best person to give advice on a regular basis.

The key factor in the coach-sportsperson relationship is trust: the coach has to know that the person he is helping takes him seriously and will act

on his advice, while the person taking the advice has to know that the coach is not simply saying the first thing that comes into his head in the hope that his pupil will go away.

CONTACT

For further information on finding a coach consult BC's website, or contact BC's coaching department on 0161-274 2065, email: **coaching@britishcycling.org.uk**

PROGRESSIVE OVERLOAD

Training to improve athletic performance in any sport is based on a simple physiological principle: as you make your body work harder over time, so it adapts to the increased workload and becomes more efficient. The aim of training is to force your body into a series of repetitions of the following cycle: exertion—fatigue—recovery—compensation.

You train, you get tired, you recover; then, because you have forced your body to function more efficiently, you can train harder. The cycle will be repeated again and again as your body becomes used to the efforts necessary to go further and faster while recovering more quickly.

The emphasis in training has to be on the word "progressive" as much as on the word "overload". Hence the need to plan your training on a daily basis, and the vital importance of keeping an objective record over the days and weeks so that you can analyse when to increase the load, and when to back off.

It's dangerous to assume that if you simply go out every day and bash yourself into submission, your body will adapt and you will improve. In fact, your body will rebel, and you will either have to rest or get ill. This is unpleasant, and the time lost will mean that you improve more slowly.

There is another trap to avoid: when your body has compensated after training at a higher level, you will find riding at that level easier and you will be tempted to stay there. That might mean, for example, that you have gone out for a series of rides at 20 miles per hour, or 75 per cent intensity — you've suffered and then recovered. Eventually, as your body gets used to the pace, the temptation is to continue riding at that intensity. You will still improve, but not as quickly as if you increase the speed by half a mile per hour, or move up to 80 per cent.

WEEK 4 JANUARY 25 2004

Pulse/Waking: 50   Weight: 80kg

Feel-Good: 5   Sleep: 9 hours

Diet: Breakfast — Cereal and Toast
Lunch — soup,
     Chicken salad,
     Rice Pudding
Dinner — Pasta and sauce,
     Fruit Salad

Training: Aim: 2hr @ level 2 (92 mins, 40 sec achieved); 10 mins level 3 (58 kilometres)

Comments: Circuit: Barton — Kimpton — Lee — Purville. Rode over Purton Hill in 52 x 21. Felt strong.

This sample page from a training diary shows a fit rider doing a hard outing

THE TRAINING DIARY

It is vital to keep a record of your training. This means you can look back when training has gone right — you have met your objectives — or wrong, resulting in illness or lack of form, and work out what can be repeated or avoided in future. There are other factors that affect you: your diet and health and "life events" — exams, a change of job, moving house. Having a record also increases your awareness of what you are doing, and enhances your motivation to keep doing it. It's also handy when consulting your coach. Hence the training diary: what should you note down?

OBJECTIVES

You should write down your goals: long-term (three to four years), medium-term (single season) and short-term (four- to eight-week training phase within a season). Then they are there in black and white. You can always come back and revise them — but record why you have done so.

How much space you take up with daily information is up to you, but the following headings are the most useful:

TRAINING

Write down what you set out to achieve — time at a given intensity — and what you actually did, plus how you felt, any pulse-monitor statistics, and other factors, e.g. weather, company, gears used, distance and time.

What you ate and drank during a ride is important as this will help you find out what works best for you. You will find it useful for future planning to note down your route — you may want to go back to a particular circuit for a particular kind of training.

PULSE RATE

Your pulse rate taken when you wake up in the morning is an important indicator of your general well-being, although it is not the only one. The pulse is easily distinguished either on the left side of the wrist as you hold the palm of your left hand up to your face, or the left-hand side of the neck.

You will soon notice trends, depending on your state of fatigue or health, and you should always look out for sudden significant variations — more than about 10 beats per minute up or down may well herald impending illness or indicate that you are fatigued and should rest.

WEIGHT

You should find that, as you get fitter, your weight gradually drops. Sudden decreases in weight may well be a symptom of dehydration. It's not necessary to weigh yourself every day, although if you're trying to lose a bit of weight it may help focus your attention on what you are eating. Once every two or three days should be enough, and try to weigh yourself at the same time of day.

"FEELGOOD" FACTOR

Nothing to do with politics, this is recommended by the Olympic cycling trainer Peter Keen. It seems incongruous but is perfectly simple: how you feel physically and mentally on a scale from six (absolutely brilliant) to one (don't want to get out of bed and face the world). You should also note outside factors that affect how you feel, such as long hours or stress at work. By comparing this over a period of time with your waking pulse rate, you should end up with a good idea of how long you need to recover from a given training session or a race.

DIET

What you eat, and what you drink, has more of an effect on how you feel and how you train than most people imagine. It's particularly important to record if you are trying to lose weight – if you have to lose weight again in future you will know just what works for you.

SLEEP

Getting enough sleep for your body to recover from training or racing is vital, but so is getting enough sleep beforehand to permit you to train or race as you want. By noting down how many hours you have slept, and comparing this with pulse rate, feelgood factor and your training records, you will recognize trends and work out how many hours you need. You will also learn to anticipate the effect of, say, a late night in the office or a night spent nursing a teething child.

USING A PULSE MONITOR

While you can assess what level you are training at by analysing how hard you are breathing and how your legs feel, a more reliable index is your current pulse rate compared to your maximum pulse rate. You can take your pulse as you ride along by feel, counting the beats for 15 seconds and multiplying by four, but it's not that accurate.

Pulse monitors with accuracy comparable to the measuring devices used by hospitals to measure heartbeat are available from about £70 to £200, and for the price you can't get a better training aid. The most sophisticated and expensive pulse monitors can be linked to a computer to provide a time/pulse-rate graph for a given ride.

This means you can see how much time has been spent in a given zone, and you can compare work rate for rides over the same route at different times. This, however, is sophistication beyond the needs of most cyclists. So too are the special sets of cranks (SRM) used by many professionals, which measure heart rate, speed and power output. Power output is the best indicator when it comes to measuring how hard you train, but there is a point when you can have too much data.

Even with the most basic pulse monitor, however, the continual read-out of your pulse rate means you have a rough indication of what intensity your body is working at, once you have figured out the relationship between your heart rate and the way you feel.

Ideally, you should try to buy a pulse monitor that can be pre-set to record how much time you spend with your heart rate in a given target zone, which will equate to whichever of the four levels of training is incorporated in your training for a given day (described in the next chapter).

In fact, a pulse monitor that will tell you the time spent within one pulse bracket will in effect give you three "zones", as usually it will also record the time spent above and below the two pulse rates. For example, if you want to train at between 140 and 165 beats per minute, you pre-enter 140 and 165, and the pulse monitor will record time below 140 beats, between the two, and over 165: three pulse "brackets" for the price of one.

It is important to note that everyone has a different maximum heart rate and different pulse rates correspond to different levels of training for different people. So don't try to train at the same pulse rate as a friend: it's fun to compare but ultimately it doesn't mean a great deal.

Clearly, when you are training with a pulse monitor – or trying to train at high intensity without one – there will be factors such as hills, descents, road junctions and traffic that will drive your pulse over the desired level or which will pull it under. So try to plan your route to

Ergometer assessments are now standard for most elite riders. Here Australia's Phil Anderson has his levels checked

include a minimum of disruption — another reason to write down routes in your training diary.

REST AND RECOVERY

When planning your training week by week, and day by day, the element that must never be overlooked is rest, to permit your body to recover and "fight back" by adapting to the increased demands you are making on it. Insufficient rest will mean that you will be unable to cope with the prescribed workload, and, at worst, you will get ill and your training will lose momentum.

The more seasons you spend racing and training, the better you will get to know your body — you will find it easier to anticipate how much time you take to get over a given type of training session, and you will be more aware of the effect that diet and factors in your lifestyle such as work and sleep have on your recovery.

The training diary is of vital importance in aiding this learning process, as it enables you to compare your training, lifestyle and diet with indicators of your health and well-being. Trends of low recovery from training or of good recovery will soon become clear.

The most obvious sign is the "feelgood factor". If this descends consistently, beware. Look out for listlessness, irritability, unwillingness to train, difficulty in sleeping, and a tendency to put off small tasks like cleaning the bike and paying bills. These are all signs that you may be pushing yourself too hard. Having a coach will help here. As an objective person who can assess the various events in your life, assess your physical feelings and who knows the training you have been doing, a coach should be able to prevent you doing further damage.

Resting pulse is an equally important indicator. It should slowly descend over a period of months as your heart and lungs become more efficient, then bottom out at an optimum rate. If it rises slowly from the normal rate over a few days, you are probably not recovering well. You can expect it to be slightly higher the day after a hard session or a race, but you should not be looking to train hard on such days anyway. You should also watch out for sudden increases or decreases of five beats or more, which may be a sign of extreme fatigue.

Riding with a pulse monitor over a period of time should make you aware of the feeling in your body at different pulse rates and levels of effort. A lower training pulse (around 10 beats, perhaps) than you would expect for a given effort, or difficulty in raising the pulse rate without more discomfort in the legs than you are used to, is a clear sign that you are still feeling the effects of your previous session, and you should reduce the difficulty of the ride or rest.

A significantly higher pulse than normal for a given effort is also a danger sign. On the bike, you should know within 20 minutes whether you are "OK" or not — assess how you feel, how easily the pedals turn, how aggressively you want to tackle a hill. It can be a good idea, each time you go out, to compare your feelings and pulse rate over a certain hill near the start of your ride. If the pulse rate refuses to go up and your legs feel grim, do a recovery ride instead of something more demanding.

You have to be motivated and single-minded to undertake progressive overload training, but you must not let this blind you to the need to rest and find variety in your life. If the physical signs are that you have overtrained, rest — and this means mental R'n'R as well. Go and do something different, but physically undemanding, and get a good night's sleep or two, or three.

DON'T BE AFRAID TO OBEY YOUR BODY AND TAKE A DAY OFF. Then, look back, work out why you are fatigued, and adjust your future plans accordingly.

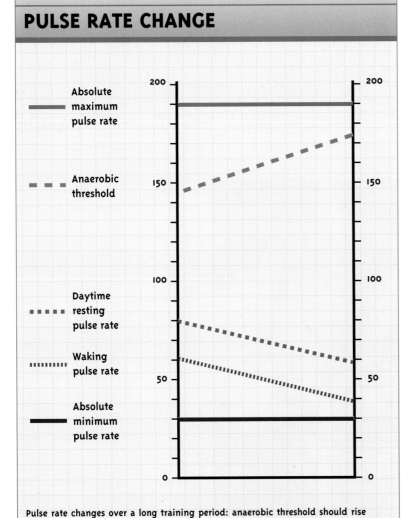

PULSE RATE CHANGE

Absolute maximum pulse rate

Anaerobic threshold

Daytime resting pulse rate

Waking pulse rate

Absolute minimum pulse rate

Pulse rate changes over a long training period: anaerobic threshold should rise slowly, resting pulse rates should decrease slowly, while absolute maximum and minimum should remain the same.

Racing to the limit of endurance, like this Italian pro has just done, takes lengthy preparation

PHYSIOLOGICAL JARGON-BUSTING

How some of the terms you will read and hear relate to what you are trying to do:

VO2 MAX

Your muscles use oxygen to burn the fuel in your muscles to produce energy. Oxygen is supplied by the lungs, which transfer it from the air to the blood, and the heart, which pumps the blood around your body. Ability to get oxygen to the muscles is the main limiting factor on athletic performance — the bulk of your training is directed towards improving it. The amount you can utilize at maximum effort is known as VO2 max, measured in millilitres of oxygen per kilogram of bodyweight per minute.

INTENSITY THRESHOLD

For efforts at low, medium and high intensity as described in the following chapter, your muscles can burn enough fuel using the oxygen brought in by the lungs and heart. This kind of effort is known as an aerobic effort. At high and maximum intensity, your muscles cannot burn oxygen quickly enough to produce the necessary energy — an anaerobic effort. Burning body fuel in this way produces a by-product — lactic acid, or lactate.

This is what creates the burning feeling in your legs when you make a really intense effort. Your body can remove the acid, and recycle it, as long as you do not produce too much of it. The point at which you produce more than you can cope with is the point at which the effort becomes intolerable — the "anaerobic threshold". Training at and beyond your anaerobic threshold is what you are doing when you do interval training. As you get fitter, the pulse rate at which you cross the threshold will rise.

SLOW- AND FAST-TWITCH

Your muscles are made up of red and white fibres. The red fibres are "slow-twitch": able to stand constant repetition of an effort over a period of time — endurance efforts. The white fibres are "fast-twitch" — for quick, short bursts of effort, producing more power over a shorter time. It should be noted that "fast-twitch" muscles can be "endurance-adapted" — trained to maintain their ability to produce a lot of power over an extended period.

The proportion of fast- and slow-twitch fibres in your muscles dictates whether you will go at a moderate speed for a long time, or a high speed for a short time. Different disciplines in bike racing demand a different proportion of each — a track sprinter, who makes a 40-miles-per-hour effort for a few seconds, will have a higher proportion of fast-twitch muscles. A Tour de France rider, making his effort at varying speeds over three weeks, will have more slow-twitch muscles, combined with enough fast-twitch to enable him to cope with the high speeds of the race. The presence of both kinds of fibre is why your training must include endurance work — slow-twitch muscle-fibre building — and training for speed and strength, building up the fast-twitch muscles.

4: ADVANCED TRAINING

YOU'RE READY TO MOVE ON FROM JUST GETTING FIT TO PREPARING FOR RACE DAY, SO IT'S TIME TO GET A BIT MORE SOPHISTICATED WHEN YOU GO OUT AND TRAIN. IT'S NOT JUST ABOUT MAXIMUM HEART RATES, POWER TRAINING, AND INTERVAL TRAINING, BUT ABOUT HOW HARD YOU ARE RIDING YOUR BIKE, AND HOW IT ALL FITS TOGETHER IN THE CYCLING YEAR.

IMPORTANT NOTE — if you are new to cycling or have not participated regularly in an endurance sport, do not attempt any of the exercises in this chapter without first getting medical assurance that you are fit to do so. This is particularly important if there is any history of heart trouble in your family or if you are under 21 or over 40.

In the early stages of cycling, before racing enters the equation, merely riding your bike further and faster and over more hills than before, sometimes in company, sometimes alone, will provide the progression that keeps you getting fitter, leaner and hungrier for more.

There comes a point, however, when you realize that merely riding your bike is not enough and it is time to progress to more focused and intense training. This point varies for every cyclist. A coach will tell you when to move forward to the type of training described in this chapter, but if you do not have a coach, be cautious. Too much intensity if you are not fully fit is counterproductive and can be dangerous.

For complete newcomers to cycling, it may take a year to get to this stage. For those who have come from other sports — running, perhaps — a couple of months' conditioning and adapting to being on a bike may suffice. Under-18s should only attempt interval training sessions similar to those described here with the guidance of a coach or a parent with knowledge of endurance sport.

The start point for increasing the intensity of your training should not be until after you have ridden a few entry-level races — club 10-mile time trials, a mountain bike enduro or two, or a fourth-category road race. Go into intensity carefully, a step at a time and do not go harder until you feel happy with what you are doing.

THE FOUR LEVELS OF INTENSITY

In order to train specifically to meet a specific end, you need to have a good idea of the level of intensity that you are trying to achieve in a given training session and what aspect of your bike racing it will improve. On the road, there are two basic ways to assess the level of the intensity at which you are riding: how close you are to your maximum pulse rate, and the way you feel.

As a rough guide to levels of intensity, imagine the following scenario. It should be stressed that the pulse measurements given below are approximate guidelines that will vary for every individual, particularly if you are an adolescent or a veteran. The "feel" of your effort is equally important as a guide.

You're riding with a friend who is a professional racer, and he has lightheartedly offered to put you through your paces. You agree, and select a long stretch of road that rises imperceptibly. Here he will gradually increase the speed, and you must try to keep alongside his front wheel.

To start with, you're chatting and continue talking as the speed rises and your heart rate slowly increases. At first you don't feel the effort and can keep talking — this is level one: low intensity, or, typically, a pulse rate up to about 45 or 50 beats below your maximum.

Gradually it becomes less easy to talk — you are taking deep, strong breaths between sentences, and you have to concentrate quite hard as you turn your legs to keep up. You're now in level two — medium intensity — with your pulse between 50 and 35 beats below its maximum.

Quite quickly it becomes impossible to talk beyond quick phrases, your legs begin to complain about the effort they are making, and you can focus on nothing but the position of your friend's wheel and the bit of road ahead. You shift position in order to be more aerodynamic. You're now in level three, and your pulse rate is between 25 and 15 beats below its maximum: this is high intensity.

Your friend (well, he was your friend a few minutes ago) accelerates again, and fatigue begins to set in. Your legs begin to feel heavy and painful. Quickly the feeling of fatigue becomes unbearable. You can't control your breathing: your heart and lungs can no longer supply all the oxygen your muscles need. Your pulse can go no higher. Very soon you have to slow down, and gulp in air to recover.

So what is going on in your body when you ride at each of the levels, and to what end can each one be used in training?

LOW INTENSITY — LEVEL ONE

- Stress on the body: minimal.
- Length of possible session at this level: indefinite.
- Limiting factors: potential dehydration, energy uptake. Aches and pains in areas such as buttocks and lower back at entry level.
- Use in training: recovery from a previous day's session for more experienced riders; increasing riding skill and getting used to the bike without making the body work too hard for entry-level riders; building stamina.
- Equivalent race effort: riding in a road-race bunch at a steady pace.
- Heart rate: from resting rate to about 45 or 50 beats per minute below maximum.

MEDIUM INTENSITY — LEVEL TWO

- Stress on the body: moderate.
- Length of possible session at this level: up to four hours at low level, but recovery takes a couple of days. Usually one to two hours.
- Limiting factors: carbohydrate supply in muscles and liver, which usually lasts up to 90 minutes.
- Use in training: fat burning; increasing heart capacity, blood volume, and muscle capillary system. Provides a "foundation" of fitness.
- Equivalent race effort: "sitting-in" in a road-race bunch that is riding quickly. Riding a long-distance time trial. Steady mountain biking.
- Heart rate: between 35 and 50 beats per minute below maximum.

HIGH INTENSITY — LEVEL THREE

- Stress on the body: intense, "at the limit" before fatigue sets in.
- Length of possible session at this level: 20 to 40 minutes for most cyclists; up to 90 minutes for the elite.
- Limiting factors: resistance to lactic acid, a waste product produced in your muscles at high intensity that causes the pain in your legs.
- Use: increasing heart strength. Effectively training your body for racing effort.
- Equivalent race effort: time-trial pace, riding on your own at sustained speed; riding in a break in a road race; climbing in a mountain-bike race.
- Heart rate: between 25 and 15 beats per minute below maximum.

NEAR MAXIMUM INTENSITY — LEVEL FOUR

- Stress on the body: the point at which you "blow up".
- Length of possible session at this level: in a trained racer, up to 90 seconds; in an untrained person, only a few seconds.
- Use: increasing short-term power and speed; replicating explosive efforts for any kind of race; resisting short-term fatigue (lactic acid tolerance).
- Equivalent race effort: making the final sprint in a road race; the final mile of a time trial; the top of the first climb in a mountain-bike race; a sprint on the track.
- Heart rate: between 10 and zero beats below maximum.

Interval training calls for quiet roads, big efforts and total concentration

EXPLOSIVE EFFORT

The four levels of training are a simple method of relating effort to the way you feel. Road, track and mountain-bike racers need another element: explosive power, such as is used in a brief sprint to respond to an attack in a road race or track event. In a short, total effort, the full pulse response will come after the end of the effort so the pulse monitor is of less use. What matters here is "feel": an explosive effort is all-out, but ends as your lungs begin to feel short of breath.

MAXIMUM HEART RATE

Most intensive training is done with the help of a pulse monitor, and to exploit this training aid to the full you need to know your personal maximum heart rate. Ideally, you should measure this in a laboratory on an ergometer, which will replicate the effects of pedalling from a steady pace to flat out, then exhaustion. A coach registered with British Cycling should be able to help set this up for you.

If you have no access to an ergometer, you can find your maximum pulse rate yourself. It's better done on your own, and must be done on a day when you are feeling good and after a warm-up of between 30 minutes and an hour. Ride on a slightly uphill or flat road, without any junctions. Begin by riding normally, then aim to increase speed by two kilometres per hour every minute.

Within 10 minutes you should reach exhaustion, and you should note the highest pulse you reach (handily, most pulse monitors have a maximum pulse read-out). It also helps if you try to get an idea of the pulse rate when you move between each of the four "zones of intensity" described in this chapter. This is because pulse rate alone is not a totally reliable measure of your work rate, merely an indicator. Your physical sensations — how hard you are breathing, how hard you have to concentrate, how much your legs hurt — are just as important.

Alternatively, find a long, dragging hill, which should take at least five or six minutes to climb. Go up at an increasingly high intensity, then at the point where you feel fatigue setting in, sprint so that you are exhausted by the top. Again, note your maximum pulse. Repeat the test within a couple of weeks to allow for any inaccuracy in your first reading.

EXAMPLES OF TRAINING AT THE VARIOUS LEVELS

In order to progress from any level of fitness, you have to train more intensely on a progressive basis, so the next question is: what kinds of training will give you the level of intensity you want? The basic principle is that the more intense the workout, the shorter it should be, and the less intense, the longer.

Low intensity: a relaxed ride on low gears; a club run in a large group. Note that most club runs will only provide this level of intensity, and you should try to use them only as relaxation: trying to maintain level two on a club run will earn you few friends.

Medium intensity: there are several ways of achieving this, which is fortunate as it is arguably the most important kind of training, being the stepping stone from merely riding a bike to riding competitively. Before you proceed to higher intensities, make sure you are happy here. Medium intensity can be attained easily on your own: you can build spells at this pace into a longer ride, with time to recover between each one. Start with about 10–15 minutes and build from there.

The following will also provide medium-intensity workouts: a steady ride in a group of four to six, with the pace shared equally — eventually, this could be done for up to four hours at the lower end of level two, and is the best way to build endurance and burn fat; a two- to three-hour mountain-bike ride over terrain that is not too technical so that you can sustain a good pace; a 90-minute group ride or "chain gang" with six to 10 riders — see the chapter on road-race training — will provide a workout at the upper end of level two, but you should be careful that things do not get too competitive or you will overcook it.

NOTE: for any ride including medium intensity work that lasts over an hour you will need to replace energy as you ride. See the next chapter for more info.

High intensity: A solo ride, ideally on undulating or windy roads to give you something to go at, will also do the trick, with about 10 minutes' warm-up followed by 20–45 minutes' riding on a bigger gear and at a higher speed. Again, start small, with perhaps eight or 10 minutes. A home trainer can also be used for a similar length of time. Such a session could be split up into four eight-minute efforts, up to three 30-minute efforts, with corresponding rest periods.

A club evening 10-mile time trial is a good high-intensity workout; so is a more competitive "chain gang" on flat roads where you replicate road race speed, but still have time to recover between each effort; a long mountain

climb of the type found in the Alps and Pyrenees would be another suitable high-intensity workout.

Maximum intensity: You can't sustain this for long, which means you have to allow yourself time to recover after each effort. This is known as interval training, and can be done either on the road, or the home trainer.

It should be borne in mind that if you are riding road races frequently, you will be producing efforts close to your maximum as you race. It may be that, until you achieve a high level of fitness, you are getting sufficient workouts at this level to make interval training in the week counterproductive. A midweek circuit

Mountain bike racing requires a combination of explosive efforts, long spells at anaerobic threshold, and downhill skill

race, or a hard chain gang session, may be more than sufficient.

Explosive power: Typically, a power session involving a five- or 10-seconds maximum sprint with three minutes recovery, repeated 10–20 times. Can be done on the turbo, or on the road, where a short circuit relatively free of traffic is best. Road and track racers love these; time triallists tend not to.

INTERVAL TRAINING

Not many cyclists like interval training, but once you have developed a base of fitness it should be done to increase your body's ability to produce speed and to develop your resistance to fatigue, or rather the lactic acid in your muscles that makes them feel fatigued.

You shouldn't begin interval training until your body has been tuned up with plenty of level two and level three training: you will do yourself more harm than good. If you can't cope with it, continue with sessions at level three. And you must allow plenty of time for recovery after each session — at least 24 hours. Next day, do a level one ride, or rest up. It may take you 48 hours to recover completely.

The general term "interval training" is used to describe a series of repeated efforts at near-maximal intensity, with recovery periods in between each effort. It is best done with a pulse monitor to help you assess your recovery. When the pulse refuses to fall to the level it has in the previous recovery periods, or to rise to the level it has in the previous intervals, you have ceased to recover between each effort and you should stop if you have not reached the end of the session.

Repeat, or recovery training consists of a number of short-timed efforts, when you permit your body complete recovery in between each one — the pulse should go within 10 beats of your maximum by the end of the interval, then drop to about half its maximum during the recovery period. The best example would be explosive effort sessions.

Interval training properly refers to a number of short efforts when complete recovery does not take place between each one — the pulse goes within 10 beats

of maximum, or to maximum by the end of the interval, then drops to about 65 per cent of maximum during the recovery period. This replicates, for example, the period in a road race when attacks are made one after another, or a series of short, sharp climbs in a mountain-bike race.

Alternate training, referred to by Bernard Hinault's trainer Paul Köchli, is a series of timed efforts with a longer spell between each one for recovery, e.g. three minutes effort, eight minutes recovery at level two, effectively similar to the pattern of a road race, where attacks will be followed by a lull and so on, or a mountain-bike race with climbs, descents and flat sections.

NOTES ON INTERVAL TRAINING

It is important that, as a general rule, you only attempt interval training when you are free from fatigue. It is crucial that you stop a session when you begin to lose "form" — when your shoulders sag, you are unable to maintain speed, and you have to get out of the saddle. A rough guideline is that if you can't complete two efforts in a row at the desired intensity, call it a day.

The time and intensity of your intervals is something only you can work out, ideally with the assistance of your coach, to whom you should explain the weaknesses that have appeared in racing. These could include the inability to hang on to a lined-out bunch, inability to work in a breakaway group, inability to sustain a time trial pace, or "blowing up" halfway up a big climb in a mountain bike race. Together you should be able to work out the intensity and duration you need in your workouts in order to solve the problem. Short efforts can be done in sets of five or six, with a break, then another set.

From the examples given above, it may seem as if interval training only has reference to road or track racers, who have to produce efforts that are more broken up than those in time trials or mountain-bike racing. This is not the case. By improving your performance at maximum and sub-maximum intensity you will increase your ability to ride at high intensity on your own and hence improve your time trialling.

Two other things should be borne in

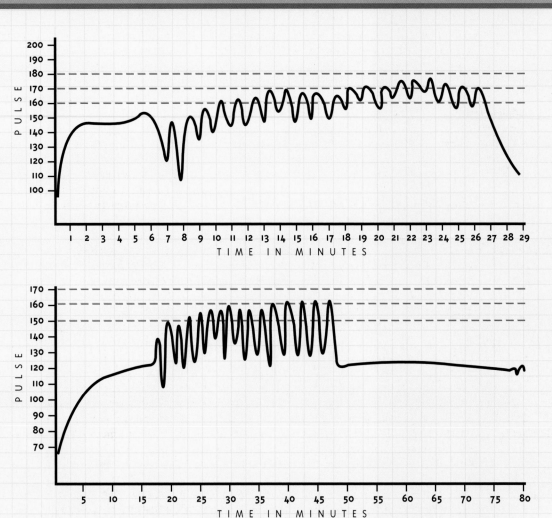

The top graph shows the pulse rate and time (in minutes) from the pulse monitor of a rider doing a relatively brief interval training session, including warm-up and warm-down, clearly showing the pulse falling during each brief recovery session. The rider's maximum pulse rate is just under 180 beats per minute, and he takes a while to reach it.

The bottom graph shows the pulse rate and time (in minutes) from the pulse monitor of a rider doing a longer interval training session, including lengthy warm-up and a period of steady warm-down afterwards. This rider was making all-out efforts of about 15 to 20 seconds.

mind. You can mix different types of intervals for variety — if you are training for road or track racing this is not a bad idea, as things never happen that precisely. If you do, be careful that you make your body work in the correct metabolic order — for example, if you do 10 one-minute sprints for lactic acid tolerance, a sustained threshold session afterwards may feel hard, but you will not be training your threshold, because of the effort you have made already. As a general rule, the sessions should increase in intensity. Try to ensure that the first session will not prevent you doing the second session — if the pulse response is abnormal, stop.

You should also look to increase your workload progressively once you feel you are on top, relatively speaking, adding an extra set of repetitions, increasing the length of the effort by a few seconds, or decreasing the recovery time. To measure your progression, you should record the length, intensity and pulse rates achieved as accurately as possible.

TRAINING INDOORS

Interval training where you are going up to level four, and sustained intensity training of the type required at level three, is not always easy to do on the road. Dark evenings are not the most suitable time to go out and train hard, while the efforts you make cannot be controlled as easily on the open road as they can on an indoor trainer. The advantage of a home trainer is that you can simply get on and train, whatever the weather.

There are two types of home trainer

SPECIFIC INTERVAL PROGRAMMES

EXPLOSIVE POWER

HIGH INTENSITY, SHORT DURATION. Replicates responding to an attack in a road or track race; the start in a time trial; "attacking" a hill on the mountain bike.

PROGRAMME 1

Intensity	Maximal uphill sprint
Duration	5 seconds
Recovery	3 minutes, riding lightly
Repetitions	8–15
Sets	1
Comments	You should use a gear that can be turned over easily without labouring — aim for a "snappy" start to the sprint.

PROGRAMME 2

Intensity	Maximal sprint, moderate gear (e.g. 52x17)
Duration	10 seconds
Recovery	3 minutes
Repetitions	10–20
Sets	1
Comments	From a rolling start, launch an "all-out" sprint for 10 seconds.

INTENSITY THRESHOLD

THIS WILL STRESS YOUR ABILITY TO SUSTAIN HIGH INTENSITY FOR PROLONGED PERIODS. In other words when riding in a road-race break, or climbing a long, steep hill in a bunch, racing in a time trial, or climbing a long hill on the mountain bike. Primarily you will be trying to deal with the accumulation of lactic acid, which must be recycled by the body, or removed from the muscle.

PROGRAMME 1

Intensity	At your intensity threshold — roughly 85 per cent maximum heart rate.
Duration	8 minutes
Recovery	6 minutes
Repetitions	4
Sets	1
Comments	Can be done effectively on a turbo trainer, but ensure an adequate warm-up.

PROGRAMME 2

Intensity	Just below (2–3 beats) your threshold.
Duration	20 minutes
Recovery	12 minutes
Repetitions	1–3, depending on form
Sets	1
Comments	A hard on-the-road session, best done on rolling terrain.

AEROBIC POWER

A SESSION TO STIMULATE YOUR HEART TO IMPROVE ITS ABILITY TO TRANSPORT OXYGEN TO MUSCLES THAT ARE WORKING HARD.

Intensity	Above threshold — near maximal
Duration	3 minutes
Recovery	3 minutes
Repetitions	6
Sets	1
Comments	You must pace the effort to ensure that you are able to sustain the right intensity for the whole of each interval.

LACTIC ACID TOLERANCE

A PAINFUL SESSION WHOSE AIM IS TO DEVELOP TOLERANCE TO THE PAIN ASSOCIATED WITH THE BUILD-UP OF HIGH LEVELS OF LACTIC ACID.

Intensity	Maximal
Duration	45 seconds
Recovery	3 minutes
Repetitions	8
Sets	1
Comments	You must ride through the pain. Do not allow pedal revs to drop, or shift into a lower gear. Best done on a long drag or flat road; also great on a turbo trainer.

MUSCLE POWER

AIMED AT DEVELOPING MUSCULAR STRENGTH NECESSARY TO "DRIVE" A BIG GEAR OVER A HILL IN A TIME TRIAL OR MOUNTAIN-BIKE RACE, OR UP TO THE FINISH IN A ROAD RACE.

PROGRAMME 1

Intensity	On a slight incline — in the saddle, high gear, high pedal revs (75–85 per minute)
Duration	30 seconds
Recovery	2 minutes
Repetitions	6
Sets	2
Comments	Stay seated, sit back in the saddle, and "push" the pedals over hard.

PROGRAMME 2

Intensity	On a steep hill — high gear, maximum effort, low pedal revs (55–65 per minute).
Duration	12 seconds
Recovery	1 minute
Repetitions	8
Sets	1
Comments	Try to keep your upper body from moving and "assisting" the legs. Keep still on the bike and use your leg strength to climb — a sustained acceleration rather than an explosive effort.

available. The older type, known usually as "rollers", is just that: a pair of rollers for the back wheel and a single roller for the front, mounted on a frame and joined by a belt so that the wheels turn together. The problem with these is that you have to balance upright with no support, which takes practice. In addition, they offer no resistance, so it takes little effort to achieve a good speed: this means they are of little value as an aid.

A far better bet is the more sophisticated "turbo trainer", even if it is more expensive. Here, your back wheel is held tight into a tripod frame in contact with a small roller that drives a weighted flywheel, providing resistance. Your front wheel sits on the ground and does not turn. In some models you can adjust resistance as you work at a greater intensity.

A garage, or a room without central heating, is the best place for turbo training — because of the lack of cooling breeze that rushes past you when you are out on the road, you will sweat buckets. An electric fan to cool you off somewhat is recommended, as your body temperature will rise, and if you do not cool off you will get the impression that you are working harder than you actually are. To prevent your bike being corroded, cover the top tube and the point where the stem goes into the frame with an old towel to stop the sweat. Some riders like to watch television or listen to music. If you are interval training, you probably won't notice, but if you are trying a sustained level three workout some distraction might help.

The advantage of an indoor trainer is that you can alter your effort more precisely than on the road, so you can hit your pulse targets for a set of intervals more easily. But the same ground rules should apply as for training on the road — when you can't hit the level you want, or recover as fast as you want to or expect to, stop. And make it progressive — gradually add time to the interval, and cut the recovery time as you get fitter.

BUILD-UP AND PEAK

So how do all these elements fit together in terms of bringing you to fitness for a racing season which, in most cases, begins in early April and goes on until October?

The general pattern followed by most cyclists from amateur time triallists to seasoned professionals is one that begins with steady, long-distance workouts to

burn body fat and build general endurance during the winter, peaking in distance terms in early spring.

Simultaneously, several weeks before racing starts, an element of extra intensity is introduced — usually, in Britain, with level three sessions on the turbo trainer. In the early season, racing is seen as bringing in a welcome extra element of intensity, rather than as an end in itself.

As the weather improves during spring, the emphasis changes to shorter, more intense workouts, with interval training gradually introduced into the programme. With lighter evenings in summer, "chain gangs" and midweek races start, giving the opportunity for intense workouts in company without the mental effort of interval trainingo.

Many cyclists approach their seasons in a haphazard way, "getting the miles in" over the winter, then going straight into early season races and simply racing through the season without any great idea of where they are going.

A better approach is to work out when you want to hit peak fitness, then count back in four-week periods, building in intensity towards your goal or goals. This can only be done once you have established your goals, and once you have an idea of the kind of workload you can cope with, and the kind of workouts that improve your weak areas. The final four weeks should concentrate on short, high-intensity workouts, with plenty of rest so that you don't overdo it.

The previous four-week period should be seen as a transition between longer, medium-intensity work and the high-intensity sessions of the final build-up. Races can and should be used as part of the build-up, as intensive workouts and as "rehearsals" for key events.

The aim is to produce a "final taper" in training before the target event, reducing the frequency and duration of training sessions, but maintaining the intensity. The idea is that this will allow your body to recover from the efforts made in the preceding week. It will "overcompensate", and hopefully this will produce a peak in your form. Over several seasons, a well-kept training diary will enable you to assess the success with which you can peak for a given race.

5: EATING FOR SPEED

WAY BACK WHEN, ALL CYCLISTS WERE EXPECTED TO EAT WAS A RARE STEAK WITH SOME HARD-BOILED RICE, AND IT HAD TO BE SITTING IN YOUR STOMACH THREE HOURS BEFORE THE FLAG DROPPED. THAT'S ALL CHANGED. WELCOME TO THE WORLD OF SOLUBLE CARBOHYDRATE DRINKS, PROTEINS, VITAMINS, EATING TO LOSE WEIGHT, AND — VITALLY — AVOIDING THE BONK.

All top cyclists have their nutritional preferences. Greg LeMond, three times a winner of the Tour de France, was legendary for eating Mexican food and the occasional hamburger. Jacques Anquetil, five times a winner of the Tour, was noted for his liking for the odd bottle of champagne, while Robert Millar took the King of the Mountains jersey in the Tour on a vegetarian diet, with a frequently avowed love of Cadbury's creme eggs and milk chocolate.

These three examples illustrate a key fact that is often forgotten: eating for speed need not be a penance, but should instead be a matter of balance. It is better to allow yourself the occasional departure from what is recommended than to stick rigidly to a diet for several weeks then go to the opposite extreme. LeMond, Anquetil and Millar could permit themselves the occasional delicacy because over years of careful eating they had worked out what and how much of a given food would or would not affect their performance.

The old truism "you are what you eat" does not quite apply to sportspeople: what you eat will not make you a super performer — that is predetermined by your physical and mental make-up. But healthy eating will help you recover more quickly from a race or training session and improve your resistance to disease and fatigue that may prevent you racing and training.

Changing or improving the quality of the food you consume should be a gradual process, which eventually will become a habit, rather than a rigid imposition that it becomes sinfully pleasurable to subvert. Eating a healthy diet need not be boring or cranky — vary what you eat, and how you eat it, and invest in a couple of good recipe books. Although you may be restricted by what your family wants to eat, most of the points made here will also benefit non-athletes. Firstly, however, we should work out why athletes eat what they do.

THE DIFFERENT KINDS OF FOOD WE EAT

We eat food for three reasons — to provide the energy we consume to stay alive; to build and repair the body; and to enable the various bits of the body to function efficiently.

Energy for intense physical effort comes principally from carbohydrate, which is stored in the liver and muscles in the form of glycogen. Carbohydrate appears in the diet in three forms: natural sugars — for example fruits and their juices; refined sugars — for example jam, honey and soft drinks; and starches, also known as complex carbohydrates, found in foods like potatoes, pasta and bread for example.

The body's other major source of energy is in the fat that is stored around the body. Fat has a higher energy density than carbohydrate, which means that per gram it supplies more fuel: it is estimated that if all the energy stored in the fat reserves of a lean, 70-kilogram bike rider were there as glycogen, he would weigh about 123 kilograms. Most people have enough fat in their bodies to fuel many hours of activity, which means there is no need to eat fat in any great quantity, particularly as any excess carbohydrate or protein is converted to fat and stored for future use.

Proteins play the major role in building up and repairing the body: they are found in meat, fish, eggs and dairy products, in vegetables such as beans, lentils and peas, and also in carbohydrate-rich foods such as bread and potatoes. In extreme situations, protein is also burned to produce energy.

Vitamins and minerals enable the body's processes to function normally. For example, Vitamin A is important for maintaining the skin, helping resist infection and maintaining good eyesight. One source of the vitamin is carrots — indicating that there may be some truth in the old saw that carrots help you see in the dark. Fruits, vegetables, fish and dairy products, meat and eggs are all important sources of various vitamins.

The final element is fluid. The body can function for some time without solid food by running off stored energy and protein, but without water, a vital part of all bodily processes, death soon results. A drop in your body water, through sweating, of just 2 per cent will reduce your performance, 5 per cent will cause fatigue and 10 per cent could be fatal. For this reason, it is vitally important to make sure that you take on sufficient fluid when training and racing.

WHAT YOU NEED TO EAT

All four elements in your diet are important to you as a cyclist. Your intake of energy providers is vital if you are not to run out of the "fuel" stored in the muscles and liver. Body repair materials are equally important if you are to rebuild the muscle fibres you break down as you train, and if you are to construct stronger ones, which is the whole point of training. Serious vitamin or mineral imbalance, or dehydration, will lead to illness and loss of performance.

Because endurance athletes such as cyclists are so much more active than other people, sports scientists recom-

Eating on the move is a vital skill: here Lance Armstrong shows how it is done

mend that their diets should include a relatively large proportion of carbo-hydrate to supply the fuel for all this activity. The recommended proportions are 60–70 per cent of calories from carbohydrate, 15 per cent of calories from protein, and 15–30 per cent of calories from fat.

This means that it is important to know the relative carbohydrate, protein and fat content of what you are eating on a daily basis. This information is helpfully included on the packaging of most foods. A 250 gram packet of spinach pasta, for instance, contains 138 grams of carbohydrate, 30 grams of protein, and 4.5 grams of fat.

The actual energy supplied by food is measured in kilocalories, the measure-ment usually used by nutritionists to express recommended daily energy intake: 1 gram of carbohydrate provides 4 Kcal; 1 gram of protein 4 Kcal; 1 gram of fat 9 Kcal. Thus the carbohydrate in the above packet of pasta provides 552Kcal of energy; the protein 120Kcal and the fat 40.5Kcal.

You could take the considerable time necessary to sit down and work out precisely how much of everything you are eating, but this is impractical for most people: it's better to look quickly when you are in the supermarket, and get an idea of what the relative proportions are. This information will help you to identify foods that will give you the carbohydrate and protein you need without giving you too much fat at the same time. For example, pasta is well known as an excellent high-energy, low-fat food, and this is reflected in the figures above.

FOOD FOR THOUGHT

NOURISHING CARBOHYDRATE-RICH FOOD

- Wholemeal bread, bagels, muffins, wholemeal biscuits, breakfast cereals – oats, wheatflakes, cornflakes.
- Brown rice and other grains.
- Potatoes.
- Sweetcorn.
- Fresh fruit, fruit juice, dried fruit.
- Peas, beans, lentils.
- Pasta and noodles.
- Milk and yoghurt.
- Crispbreads and rice cakes.

Foods that are rich in refined sugars, such as those listed below, are also sources of carbohydrate, but in many cases they may have been refined to the extent that they have lost many of their other nutrients.

- Sugar and syrups.
- Jam, marmalade and honey.
- Soft drinks.
- Sweets and chocolate.
- Biscuits, cakes and scones.
- Ice cream.
- Puddings.
- Sports drinks containing glucose, sucrose or glucose polymers.

FOODS RICH IN VITAMINS AND/OR MINERALS

- Fresh fruit and berries, and their juices.
- Dried fruits.
- Vegetables – particularly green, leafy vegetables.
- Liver and kidneys.
- Fish oils, such as cod liver and halibut oil.
- Eggs.
- Milk and dairy products.
- Wholegrain bread and cereals.
- Pulses – beans, lentils, peas.
- All kinds of fresh, salted and roasted nuts and seeds, e.g. sesame.

LOW-FAT, HIGH-PROTEIN FOODS

- Peas, beans, soya, lentils, Quorn.
- Chicken, turkey, veal and game.
- Skimmed and semi-skimmed milk, yoghurt, and low-fat cheeses, e.g. cottage cheese, fromage frais.
- Grilled, baked or poached fish.
- Lean trimmed beef.

CARBOHYDRATE

Carbohydrate intake has the most immediate bearing on your performance and your recovery from training. Just 90 minutes of continuous intense exercise can lead to the exhaustion of the glycogen stores in the muscles and liver. As it can take up to 36 hours to replenish the glycogen stores, or longer, it is clear that if you are to exercise intensely on a daily basis you must eat sufficient carbohydrate to keep the glycogen stores topped up. Insufficient carbohydrate intake will lead to poor recovery and poor performance.

As cyclists are recommended to eat a high proportion of their daily food intake as carbohydrate, it is important to choose carbohydrate-rich foods that are also high in other nutrients so that sufficient amounts of vitamins, minerals and protein are consumed at the same time. As a general rule, foods containing natural sugars and starches, rather than refined sugars, have a high content of both energy and nutrients: for examples of such foods, a variety of which should make up the bulk of your diet, see box above.

This means that they should not be used as substitutes for the nutrient-rich carbohydrate sources listed, around which your diet should be based. They can be used to boost carbohydrate intake without putting too much bulk into the stomach, but you must bear in mind that most biscuits, cakes and desserts have a high fat content. Refined sugars have another downside: they create a rapid influx of sugars into the body, which leads to the desire to repeat the dose. They are "more-ish" and as you are likely to be attempting to control your weight, they are not recommended in any quantity.

It is important to look for sweet food that will give you rapid, concentrated carbohydrate when you need it – for example when you come into the house after a hard ride, or during a long ride – but without too much sugar or fat. Malt loaf, semolina, rice pudding, creme caramel, bananas and fig rolls are old favourites among endurance athletes.

PROTEIN

Protein-rich foods provide the range of substances known as amino acids, which the body uses mainly to repair and build muscle – vitally important for the athlete, as during training you are constantly causing minute damage to the muscle tissues, which has to be "rebuilt". It is estimated that endurance athletes need to take in 1.2 to 1.4 grams of protein per kilogram of bodyweight per day. So an 80-kilogram cyclist will need between 98 and 112 grams of protein per day.

Proteins are found in a wide variety of foods, making protein supplements rarely necessary for cyclists. As with carbohydrate, food labelling information can be used when shopping to help you select high-protein, low-fat foods.

While cyclists are not as reliant on red meat now as in the days when folklore stipulated that a raw steak be eaten before every race, vegetarians have particular needs. In order to get a full range of amino acids in their diet, they should be careful to combine different kinds of protein-rich products such as beans, chickpeas, lentils and cereals. Low-fat dairy products such as semi-skimmed or skimmed milk and low fat cheese or yogurt can also be added to meals to up the protein content.

It is worth bearing in mind that dairy and meat products that are protein-rich – and in many cases contain useful vitamins and minerals – can also contain large quantities of fats. Select skimmed and semi-skimmed milk or low-fat alternatives, and lean cuts of meat.

VITAMINS AND MINERALS

All the foods recommended in the box above contain some of the vitamins and minerals that you need to keep your body in perfect working order. You should note that cooking and storage lessens the vitamin content, so you will get more vitamins from fresh, raw fruit and vegetables. Dried fruits such as apricots and raisins are also recommended by dieticians for their high mineral content.

EATING TO BE HEALTHY

From what I have said above, it follows that instead of "empty calories" — foods that are high in sugar and fat, but low in nutritional value — you should aim to eat foods that have been processed as little as possible, and thus retain more of their vitamin and mineral content. Another advantage with unprocessed and organic products is that they have had fewer or no artificial additives such as colourings, preservatives and flavouring added to them.

The bulk of your diet should thus be made up of fresh fruit, salads, wholemeal bread and pasta (rather than their processed equivalents), fruit juice, wholegrain breakfast cereals, brown rice rather than white, and lightly boiled or steamed vegetables rather than tinned ones. And if you love cakes and biscuits, go for home-baked ones made with wholemeal flour and dried fruit rather than something straight out of a packet.

You must also be careful about foods that are in themselves healthy, but are cooked in fat — particularly fried meat, chips and fish. Try alternative ways of cooking that are less fatty and actually retain the flavour of meat and fish better than frying, such as grilling, poaching and baking.

Most trainers recommend that their athletes try to cut down their intake of alcohol, tea and coffee, in spite of the major part they play in the Western diet. All three are diuretics, and will cause you to become dehydrated if you don't drink other liquids to compensate. You should avoid them in particular after a race or a hard training session, when you are dehydrated, for the same reason that you avoid them when you are ill: your body is working hard enough anyway to get you back to normal, and doesn't need the additional stress of coping with toxins.

Other foods that may be worth avoiding, particularly when you are recovering from a race or a tough training session, are "rich" or very spicy items such as curries: your stomach may find them hard to cope with when what it wants is easily absorbed carbohydrate. Professional team managers advise their riders not to eat chilled foods such as ice cream after a race, because they can affect the body's temperature mechanisms.

EATING TO LOSE WEIGHT

One of the biggest enemies of the aspiring bike racer is excess body fat. It's not the only item in the equation, but once you've got your body engine tuned up, if you can shed a few pounds from the chassis you will notice a difference as you go up any hill.

You should find that as you ride your bike for longer hours at higher intensity, you lose weight gradually — partly because you are burning more energy, partly because your body's metabolism is speeding up. It may be, however, that you need to become lighter a little faster. There are two basic ways to do this.

One is to increase your energy output, so that you burn up more of the fat stored around your body — that is, you spend more hours on your bike or doing other exercise. The other is to reduce your energy intake, so that you are taking in less energy in the form of carbohydrate and fat than you are putting out.

The ideal solution is a mixture of both, a combination of increasing slightly the hours you spend exercising — not necessarily through on-the-bike work — and closely focusing on what you eat, and how much you eat. Don't look upon it as "going on a diet" for a few weeks, at the end of which you will be a sylph-like bike rider. Consider it more as a gradual change in your eating habits that will bring your weight down over time. Losing more than a pound or two a week is an unrealistic target — it may be unhealthy and it may impair performance.

As well as the nutritional adjustments described early in this chapter, try some of the following:

- Avoid ready-prepared meals, which are often very high in fat and salt and at the same time low in complex carbohydrate. If you buy them, check the fat content.
- Switch from full-fat to half- or low-fat

Richard Virenque puts away a bike racer's breakfast, with cereals and fruit juice to the fore

milk and look for low-fat cheeses and spreads.
- Avoid foods that have been fried or cooked in batter or breadcrumbs.
- Snack healthily, with fruit, bread or low-fat yoghurts rather than cakes, sweets, biscuits or chocolate.
- Instead of desserts containing pastry, cream or sugar, try fresh fruit salads or low-fat yoghurt, which can be livened up with extra fruit or muesli.
- Swap from red meat to poultry or fish.
- Processed meats such as sausages, salami and meat pies are usually high in fat. Reduce your intake or stop eating them altogether.
- A lot of garnishes are fatty, so you should avoid, for example, butter on baked potatoes and bread, mayonnaise on salads. Instead of cream on desserts, use low-fat yoghurt and fromage frais.
- Drink more water.
- Slightly reduce the portions of food in your meals.
- When buying food, check the nutritional information and aim for products with a low fat-to-carbohydrate ratio.
- Weigh yourself daily, at the same time, and record your weight and what you are eating in your training diary.

VITAMIN SUPPLEMENTS

In the ideal world, if you ate a perfectly balanced diet based on the recommendations above, it would provide all the vitamins and minerals you needed. Life may not be that simple: there is evidence that athletes in training use up more B vitamins and Vitamin C than is usual, and the more you sweat, the more minerals are flushed out of your system. In addition, particularly if you are holding down a job, or attending school or college, as well as trying to find time to train, it's not always possible to eat the best food all the time, however hard you try.

Vegetarians should pay attention to the risk of deficiency in iron and the B vitamins: green vegetables, such as spinach, broccoli and cabbage and wholegrain cereals and pulses are useful sources of iron. Women cyclists should look closely at the calcium and iron in

The Tour de France peloton collects food from team helpers, but even amateurs need to learn how to grab a bottle

Snack-in-a-box time on the Giro d'Italia: gateaux are only recommended in small doses

their diet, and should try to include foods that are rich in these minerals: again, the iron-rich green vegetables and pulses, plus liver, red meat and shellfish for iron, and calcium-rich dairy products, seafood and bread.

A vitamin and mineral supplement should not be seen as a substitute for a well-balanced diet, or as an excuse to eat unhealthily, but it is useful as additional insurance against possible mild deficiency. However, remember that no matter how important the substance may appear to be for your body, large doses of individual minerals or vitamins will do more harm than good — in high doses, some can have toxic effects. Look for a multivitamin and mineral supplement containing no more than one or two times the recommended daily amount.

The most likely occasion when you may feel the need to take additional vitamins (as well as a daily multivitamin and mineral supplement) is if you have a cold or become run-down, in which case Vitamin C is held by most doctors to assist recovery. This vitamin is water-soluble, and any excess will be flushed naturally out of your body. However, high doses of Vitamin C (above 3 grams daily) have been shown to cause stomach upsets and diarrhoea, so be careful not to overdo it.

EATING BEFORE RIDING

Cycling folklore used to insist that a racer's final pre-race meal should be eaten exactly three hours before the start, whatever time of day that might be, and should consist of steak and rice. And it was just that — folklore.

What you eat before a race — and, come to that, before any training session — should be dictated by two facts: you want your muscles to be full of glycogen when you start, and you don't want lots of food sitting in your stomach when you are racing or training.

The first point means that your final big meal prior to exercising should be high in carbohydrate and relatively low in fat, which will take longer to absorb. Examples are pasta with a low-fat sauce, chicken risotto, and baked potatoes with beans or bolognese sauce.

If you are riding early in the morning, as you will be if you are doing most time trials, many road races, and most long winter clubruns, you don't want to be getting up at the crack of dawn to prepare food. This means your final carbohydrate-rich meal will be dinner the night before — not eaten too late, so that you don't go to bed with a full stomach, which may stop you sleeping.

In the morning, at least 90 minutes before your race, you can safely get away with a light breakfast — avoiding anything fatty or bulky. Moderate amounts of sugar in the pre-event meal are beneficial. A generous portion of cereal, weak tea, toast and jam, and some fruit juice — perhaps diluted — would be typical. Your stomach should not feel full afterwards by any means. You can always top up with some dilute energy drink on the way to the race.

For an afternoon or evening race, the old-timers' three-hour rule is not a bad one to stick to, although you must be careful not to eat anything too bulky that will sit heavily in your stomach as you race, and not to eat too much. A proper meal the night before will mean you don't have to worry about shovelling down huge amounts of carbohydrate on the day.

PEDALLING FUEL

Among cycling fans who visit the Tour de France there are two favourite souvenirs.

Most sought after are little cotton bags — musettes — which contain fresh supplies of energy bars and fruit and are handed up to the riders during each long stage, then jettisoned once the contents have been transferred to the jersey pockets. Almost as desirable are the drinking bottles supplied to riders in their thousands and ditched continually during each stage as soon as they are emptied. Why does all this high-speed eating and drinking take place?

Fluid replacement is the most important process. Even if you don't notice it, you are continually losing moisture from your skin as you pedal — and in cold weather you're losing it from your lungs in the form of steam. In hot weather, you will dehydrate quickly as you race or train, which results at best in a loss of efficiency, and at worst in illness. In hot weather your body can lose up to two litres of liquid an hour in sweat: you can't replace it all immediately, but you can go some way towards reducing the consequences. Remember to pay constant attention to your fluid intake as much when training as when racing.

The main rules are to drink little and often, and to start drinking well before you get thirsty — if you feel thirsty it's too late. In a road- or mountain-bike race, as soon as things get slightly easier, reach for your bottle. How much you drink while riding is a matter for the individual, but the professional racer's rule of thumb appears to be one big drinking bottle (750ml) per hour in hot weather, and one small bottle (500ml) in cold weather.

In very hot weather if you are using a carbohydrate drink (see below), it is a good idea to have a second bottle with plain water, which actually tastes more thirst-quenching when you drink it. The water can also be used to clean your face of the salt residue left behind when you sweat — this can irritate the eyes, and also actually inhibit your sweating.

Whenever a road race is stopped for any reason, riders can always be seen urinating in the hedge. This is not due to nerves, rather to the fact that their bladders are full, as they have been taking on liquid right up to the moment the race has started: good policy in cold weather as well as hot weather. Always take an extra bottle of your race drink to consume in the car on the way, and finish it off in the changing rooms.

THINGS TO DRINK WHILE RACING/TRAINING:

- Glucose polymer drinks such as Maxim/PSP/Hi5 — for events lasting over 90 minutes.
- Fluid replacement drinks such as Isostar.
- Water — for events lasting less than 45 minutes.
- Diluted fruit juices — one part juice to two parts water.
- Dilute and preferably flat cola in the final half of a race or training ride.

DRINKS TO AVOID:

- Coffee, strong tea, alcohol — all are diuretics, and will actually dehydrate you.
- Ordinary fizzy or sugary drinks — e.g. cola, lemonade.
- Undiluted fruit juices — these are too concentrated and can exacerbate dehydration in the short term. The sugars they contain are absorbed too slowly to be of great benefit in the short term.

NOTE — Before you use a drink in a race, try it out while training. And try various different kinds of drink before you settle on one. For drinks mixed from powder, follow the manufacturer's instructions for quantity and concentration — over-concentrated drink will do more harm than good. In particular, isotonic sports drinks, which contain sodium and electrolytes that assist the transfer of water to the bloodstream, as well as carbohydrate, must be mixed to the correct concentration to be effective.

FUEL REPLACEMENT

Most training and racing takes place at between 70 and 85 per cent of VO2 Max. Studies have shown that at this workrate, about 65 per cent of the energy that drives the muscles comes from burning carbohydrate and the other 35 per cent from burning fat. The energy stored in the body's muscles as glycogen will last for about one to two hours — as it becomes depleted you experience feelings of extreme fatigue, dizziness and weakness that cyclists call "the bonk" and marathon runners "the wall".

One of the aims of medium-intensity training (see Chapters 3 and 4) is to improve your body's ability to burn fat as fuel while you are racing, enabling you to "save" more muscle glycogen for when it

really matters — towards the end of the race. Taking on carbohydrate as you race, and also as you train over long distances, will help postpone the point at which your muscle glycogen diminishes to the point where you hit "the wall".

The key word here is "postpone" — the point at which you run out of fuel depends on the intensity of the effort and the extent to which you are endurance-trained as well as the amount you have eaten before the session and what you eat during it. Your aim is to ensure that "the bonk" does not happen during your race or training ride. However, if you are not trained properly or ride at too high an intensity, you will "bonk" no matter how much you eat.

It's as important to take on carbohydrate while training as it is while racing, because if you are training hard for up to 90 minutes, you will begin to run down your glycogen reserves. This can affect recovery for future sessions. If you are training hard for over 90 minutes, it becomes vital, as the last thing you want to do is get "the bonk" miles from home.

You have three options where fuel replacement is concerned: traditional solid high-energy snacks; liquid high-energy foods such as Extran, which are used by many professionals but are very expensive for the amateur racer; and carbohydrate drinks based around glucose polymers, which are increasingly popular as they enable you to take on fuel and rehydrate yourself at the same time.

In an event under one hour, you will not digest solid food in time for it to have any effect, and in any case, you should not come close to depleting your glycogen reserves. Solid food will be of benefit in any race or training session over 90 minutes, but the only situation in which you must take on solid food is during the true long-distance events, such as a stage race, or a 12- or 24-hour time trial. Most riders using the recently developed glucose polymer drinks such as Maxim, PSP and Hi5 would agree that in most short- to medium-distance races it is now a question of individual choice whether or not you take solid food. In a race situation, most riders find it easier to drink from a bottle than to eat. Many prefer to have a bottle or two of glucose polymer, with some solid food to settle the stomach.

However, there is no evidence that

carbohydrate is absorbed more efficiently as a liquid or a solid, so if you choose solid food you are not at a disadvantage as long as you take sufficient liquid as well. Race food must provide energy fairly quickly and be easy to digest, without making you feel sick. It also needs to be solid enough to stay intact in a jersey pocket and not make your fingers all yicky when you pull it out, yet not so dry that you have trouble swallowing it.

You should begin eating as soon as possible after the start of the race or long training ride — no more than 20 minutes if you are using a carbohydrate replacement drink to prevent de-hydration as well as "the bonk".

Way back when, some racers used to swear by eating sugar lumps towards the end of a race — not as dumb as it sounds, as the brain uses sugar to function, which is why when you get "the bonk" you can find it hard to concentrate.

Examples of ways to take on carbohydrate during racing/training:

- Fruit — bananas are an old favourite, while apples or oranges cut into seg-ments are particularly good in hot weather, but are not a quick source of energy.
- Chewy fruit/nut bars.
- Fig rolls — but they are dry, and crumble in the rain.
- Malt loaf cut into slices and wrapped in foil.
- Energy bars, e.g. Isostar, Power Bar.
- Glucose polymer drinks such as Hi5, Maxim, PSP.
- Concentrated liquid carbohydrate such as Extran.

IN-FLIGHT REFUELLING

If you are racing medium to long distance, particularly in hot weather, the two bottles you can carry in the cages on your bike will not be enough, and you will need to collect drink bottles from a helper beside the race route. The ideal spot is somewhere where you are going relatively slowly — a moderate hill, without a tail wind — and where you and your helper can see each other — that is, on a straight bit of road.

Your helper should stand at the roadside — NOT IN THE MIDDLE OF THE ROAD — holding the bottle towards you at a height where you can snatch it. They should NOT run, as that causes the bottle

to jiggle about, making it hard to grasp. You should keep an eye on the bottle and a cool head, and, if you are in a road race, an awareness of what those around you in the bunch are doing. Ask for a new bottle before you actually need it, or prearrange it, then things don't become fraught if you miss it and have to wait for another lap.

EATING FOR RECOVERY

When you finish a race or a hard training session, your muscle glycogen reserves will be low and you may well be very dehydrated if the weather has been windy or hot. Your body will continue working long after you have begun resting, to repair broken-down muscle tissue and flush away the waste that has built up while you have been working.

The first priority after you stop will be rehydration: drink something, and not just the tea provided by the race organizers. Tea or Coke will make you feel better due to their sugar and stimulant content, but they will actually make you feel worse long term. Instead, or as well, go for either plain water, diluted fruit juice — a good idea because of the minerals and Vitamin C it contains — or more of the energy drink you may have been taking before and during the race or training session. There are specialist protein-based recovery drinks on the market; these are recommended, but try them before you take them to a race to make sure you find them palatable.

You can tell from your urine colour if you are dehydrated: if you produce small amounts of concentrated yellow urine, you should drink at regular intervals over the next few hours. When you are producing copious amounts of dilute urine, you are no longer dehydrated. Another precaution is to weigh yourself before and after exercise in the heat: if you've dropped two or three pounds in a session, you're probably dehydrated, as it is impossible to burn off that much fat in one go.

Having dealt with your liquid needs, the next, and also fairly urgent, priority is replacing the energy stores in your muscles, and supplying protein to your muscles, which will be full of the "micro-tears" you sustain during exercise. Don't throw down copious amounts of carbohydrate-rich food

immediately after a big effort: your stomach simply won't be able to cope and you may be sick.

After you stop, eat small quantities of foods that are high in rapidly absorbed carbohydrate but not so rich and sticky that you will feel sick. Examples would be rice, bread and bagels, bananas, raisins, sweetcorn, potatoes, semi-sweet biscuits, cornflakes and Weetabix. A baked potato with a decent dollop of tuna or bolognese would combine carbohydrate and protein; white meat and ham are other good sources of easily digested protein.

According to Chris Boardman's trainer Peter Keen, research has shown that eating a small amount of carbohydrate-rich food immediately after training or racing, followed by a larger meal a couple of hours later, can dramatically improve the replenishment of your glycogen reserves. The opposite also applies — low carbohydrate intake after exercise means the "fuel tanks" will not be refilled as quickly.

Keen recommends around 300–500Kcal for this small meal. The equivalent would be half a tin of semolina or rice pudding with fruit, a medium bowl of pasta and sauce, or two or three muesli bars. It's worth planning things so that immediately after any moderately hard training session, you can eat quickly in order to speed up your recovery before the next session. Have the food ready to bung in the microwave or prepare the sandwiches before you go out.

In the book *High-Tech Cycling*, Michael Sherman suggests that an alternative would be to eat a snack of 0.4 gram of carbohydrate per kilogram of bodyweight every 15 minutes, beginning immediately after exercise. For an 80-kilogram cyclist that would work out at 32 grams of carbohydrate, or 120Kcal — a small muesli bar or a third of a tin of creamed semolina.

Wait a couple of hours if you can before eating a large meal. If you can't wait — for example, you have just ridden an evening event — eat a light meal, but make sure it includes plenty of carbohydrates. Don't race or train hard, eat a heavy meal, then go to bed. It won't be a happy experience.

Whether you're training or racing, and whatever the weather, you should always get down plenty of fluid

6: TIME TRIALLING

THE TRADITIONAL ENTRANCE POINT TO CYCLE SPORT FOR MOST BRITISH RACERS, THE "RACE OF TRUTH" OFFERS AN ADDICTIVE CHALLENGE AND ONE HUGE ADVANTAGE: BARRING INCIDENT A RESULT OF SOME KIND IS GUARANTEED. HERE'S HOW TO FIND YOUR WAY IN A DISCIPLINE WHICH STARTED OUT IN SECRET AND REMAINS THE MOST POPULAR WAY TO RACE IN BRITAIN.

The joy of time trialling is that, by and large, whenever you ride a time trial you come back with a result of some kind, which means something to you — good, bad or indifferent. In road or track racing, if you cannot handle the other riders' pace you will come home with nothing apart from sore legs and a bruised ego. In mountain-bike racing, lack of technical ability may leave you in a similar state.

At the end of a time trial, barring an act of God, you will have a time for a set distance that you can compare to times you have already done for the distance, and which you will be able to use as a point of reference in the future. You will also be able to compare it with the times of the other cyclists.

This makes this branch of cycling ideal for riders who do not have the time or the opportunity to prepare for road or track, who are just entering the sport, or who find it impossible to cope with the changes of pace or bike handling demands of a road race. You can compete, and you get something for your trouble.

Time trialling suits older riders in particular, who may be less happy with fluctuations in speed, and have greater powers of concentration. Compared to road racing and mountain-bike racing, which can take up an entire day or weekend, a time trial will usually be over quickly, leaving plenty of time to get on with the rest of your life.

Whereas a road race is a contest for the first 6, 10 or 20 places, between you and the rest, a time trial, generally speaking, is a race between you and yourself, with your friends and acquaintances entering the equation if necessary. Most riders in a British time trial are less concerned with their placing

than with the time — how does it compare to a personal best for the distance or course; is it a club record, or a useful qualifier for a club Best All Rounder competition?

The other attraction is in the technical side. What you ride in a time trial does have a bearing on your speed, so it is not surprising that riders with the wherewithal hunt down bikes and parts that may help them shave off a few seconds. That doesn't mean you need to spend a fortune, though — some of the slowest times are posted on the most expensive bikes — but it does mean that "What's that you're riding?" is a common conversational opener around the results board.

While time trials are the most accessible and convenient form of cycle sport, it should be pointed out — without in any sense attempting to do the sport down — that, for historical reasons, time trialling British-style is something of an anachronism in the greater scheme of things. Time trialling on fixed courses, located to provide the fastest possible times, does not happen anywhere else in the world.

In Europe, time trials are viewed as a key test of individual or team strength in the great stage races such as the Tour de France. The discipline has had its own official world title since 1994, and has been an Olympic sport since 1996. Courses bear no resemblance to many of those in Britain, which tend to emphasize speed: abroad, organizers go out of their way to find hills, corners, anything that will break a rider's rhythm.

There are good reasons why every cyclist should ride time trials. The ability to pace yourself when riding on your own, and the knowledge of the physical sensations that you gain from riding time trials, are vital assets in every other

branch of the sport. Mountain-bike races, after the hectic start, are essentially off-road time trials. The ability to ride alone at speed has won many a road race. The track pursuit is essentially a very short time trial: it is no coincidence that Chris Boardman combined the two disciplines, or that David Millar — world time-trial champion in 2003 — is considering doing the same.

However, if you are at a formative stage in your cycling, you should not devote yourself exclusively to the solo side of the sport. A promising junior can win British time trials week-in, week-out, then find at 19 or 20 that he has nowhere further to go, because he has not attempted road or track racing. The best time triallists, riders such as Chris Boardman, Graeme Obree and David Millar, forge successful careers in which time trials are only one significant element.

TIME TRIALLING FOR THE BEGINNER

The club 10-mile time trial is the ideal introduction to cycle racing, on a par at least with a novice's mountain-bike race as an unpressurized way into the sport. It doesn't particularly matter what kit you have — the entry fee is usually no more than £2, and the investment in mental effort and physical preparation need not be great. Some clubs will let you ride on a "race and see" basis without making you join first: your local club contact will give you a place and time, and will indicate whether or not you need to be a club member. Under-16s will need a parent to sign a parental permission form.

Full aero kit and a fancy start ramp: the world championships are time trialling's pinnacle

David Millar (no. 41) catches his minute man in the Tour of Spain and overtakes without breaking his concentration

The usual route for beginners to time trialling is to start with club 10-mile time trials, and gradually work up through club 25-mile races to "open" events. As you get fitter you should see your times gradually improving compared to those of the front runners. Entry to "open" races on popular (i.e. fast) courses is performance-related, so once you get to this stage you should ask around and seek out "middle-markers" races — events for riders of average ability — and less popular courses. Races are listed in the Cycling Time Trials handbook, and entry forms are usually available from club secretaries or the Cycling Time Trials.

PACING YOURSELF

One top time triallist describes the principle of judging your effort in a time trial as similar to that of pouring water out of a bottle. You should aim to pour steadily, gauging your pace so that as you cross the line the last drop of water, metaphorically speaking, should drip out of the bottle. If you pour too quickly to begin with, you will run out of water, so to speak, whereas if you don't pour quickly enough, you will have water to spare.

The art of pacing yourself is something you learn from experience, but some riders seem to be born with the ability. The more you time trial, the better you will know just how much you have left, and how hard you can race.

A pulse monitor will help, as it offers an insight into what is going on in your body to accompany the "feel" of the ride in your legs. Experience in racing and training will show you what pulse rate you can sustain without "blowing up". It should be about 90 per cent of your maximum, which you should have established before you begin training, or just below your anaerobic threshold — see jargon-busting at the end of Chapter 3 — "Training Principles".

What distinguishes expert time triallists is that their anaerobic thresholds are reached very close to their maximum pulse rates — in other words, for a given sustained speed they can get far closer to "blowing up" than normal human beings, and thus sustain the speed for longer. A time trial stage winner in the Tour de France — David Millar or Lance Armstrong, for example — would be able to ride a British "25" in 47 minutes, and a "10" in 18 minutes.

Unless you have done other endurance sports, particularly running, when you start time trialling you will not be able to race close to your maximum power output. You will push yourself over your threshold and blow up. As you race and train, however, your threshold should gradually rise, until you reach a limit imposed either by your physique, or by the amount of training you have time for.

SHORT-DISTANCE TIME TRIALS — 10 AND 25 MILES

Physiologically, short-distance time trials are all ridden at similar intensity — just below a rider's anaerobic threshold, or at the high end of level three on the scale of intensity. A former 10-mile record-holder describes it as "the point where you are gasping, but you can continue the effort, where you know that you aren't going to blow up in a couple of miles".

The effort required is surprisingly intense, and producing the right intensity for the right length of time is a hard skill to master. A pulse monitor helps here, once you have worked out at what pulse rate you blow up. For a "10" you need ideally to be at the top of level three — a few beats below your threshold, or just on the threshold. For a "25" you should be about 5–10 beats below. It may take a while to achieve this if you are a beginner.

The objective of training for short-distance time trialling is to accustom your body to riding continually at a very high intensity for a given length of time — up to an hour for a "25". In contrast, for road racing you are aiming to acquire bike-handling skill, and to cultivate the ability to change pace and go over your threshold for short periods of time when a situation demands it.

To ride a good time trial you don't want to go over the threshold. What this means is that your time-trial training should not be based around "short" interval training — repeated sprints — but rather around keeping up a continuous high intensity for as long as necessary.

Most short-distance time triallists split their year into three parts. Between January and March, the programme is similar to that of a road racer — plenty of miles at level one and level two to burn off fat and build stamina. This is frequently done in company, on club training rides. From mid-March until May, the build-up gains in intensity as racing at weekends — perhaps initially on alternate weekends — is introduced. Midweek training sessions are raised to racing intensity, even if only for half an hour at a time.

The emphasis here remains on "progressive" rather than "overload", with plenty of rest to allow the body to recover. Early season, when racing begins, is when racers tend to get ill as they push too hard too soon, so it is particularly important to pay attention to signs of fatigue. Many use a turbo trainer indoors to get the necessary intense training without venturing out in the cold and dark.

Midweek club time trials tend to begin when the evenings become lighter in mid-May, and from then until September, when most will have ended, it is possible to use a midweek 10- or 25-mile time trial, or two, as race training,

with a race — or two in many riders' cases — at the weekend. Training becomes irrelevant, because your racing is your training, and what riding you do outside races is purely devoted to recovery rides at level one.

The flexibility of midweek club races means that you don't have to turn up if you're tired, and the large numbers of non-starters in many weekend "open" events would suggest that entrants regard them as being equally flexible. It's better to be a little more conservative than continually register as "did not start", and it's important to aim for a balance between the stimulus of racing rather than training, and the fact that too many races will make you stale. Be selective — it's better to race twice a week, properly, than four times badly.

HOW DO I TRAIN?

A time-trial training session needs to be a sustained spell of riding at level three on flattish roads where you can maintain a good speed. The length of the session depends on your experience and strength.

A beginner will find it hard to do more than 10 minutes, while, as an extreme example, top West London short-distance rider Eddy Adkins bases his training around a daily 18-mile ride to work — and the same distance back again — at time trial pace. However, he has been doing this for 20 years — most riders would have difficulty doing this programme for even a week.

Beginners should aim to do one or two sessions a week to start with — after getting a good base of level one or two road miles, preferably in a group. After warming up for 15 to 30 minutes, push the speed up to the pace you want to race at and hold it there as long as you can, then warm down for 15 minutes. Increase the time of the session gradually over subsequent months. You will probably only be able to do this once or twice a week to start with. Allow yourself time to recover after the session — do nothing or a level one ride the next day, and monitor yourself carefully for symptoms of overtraining.

If you have the ability to hold a wheel and ride in a group, road races and club "chain gangs" (see Chapter 8, "Road Racing — Basic Skills") can be used to increase endurance and provide variety. Select fast events on flat courses.

BEFORE RACING

"Forewarned is forearmed" goes the saying and, for "open" events, you should try to look at the course on which you will be racing before you start. Preferably this should be done on the bike, but that may not be feasible or pleasant if the course is on a busy A-road, where you will race on a quiet Sunday morning. Take the car if necessary.

Crucially, make sure you know where the course goes — look at any roundabouts and slip roads. Courses are usually "out and home" — locate the point at which you will turn and come back to the finish, as "missing the turn" happens more often than you would think, and will cost you time and concentration. Look for anything that might take you by surprise in the heat of a race. Use the start sheet for the race — the Cycling Time Trials handbook will tell you nothing about where the course goes.

THE WARM-UP

Many riders do not warm up properly, and lose time because their body is not ready for the instant intense effort a time trial demands. The time lost "getting into it" will never be regained. The warm-up should be at least 15 minutes, progressively increasing to race intensity, which you should maintain for at least five minutes, finishing no more than 10 minutes before the start. The ideal is to end your five minutes when you get to the start line and are taken into the arms of the "pusher-off", then you can blast off and get into your rhythm almost immediately. It can take up to two miles to "get going" if you don't warm up properly. The other side of the warm-up is that it prepares your muscles and tendons for the intense effort. Going off without warming up can cause torn muscles, tendon inflammation and the like.

- Some riders use a turbo trainer in the race parking area to warm up on. This means you don't have to worry about other road users, other racers getting in the way as they warm up on the same road, or about getting lost or puncturing while warming up. (Don't laugh — it has happened.)
- Don't use the turbo trainer in hot weather, as you will raise your body's temperature, which will end up impairing your performance.
- If the weather is hot, it's a good idea to

drink between warming up and starting the race.

- If it's cool, you may want to wear leg- or arm-warmers initially, but the final part of the warm-up should be in what you will wear to race in.
- Warming up on the course is not recommended, as you will get in the way of riders who are racing, and traffic that is trying to avoid them.
- Some riders warm up on training wheels with heavier tyres, then change wheels before racing, so that the bike then feels "faster". It's a nice psychological trick, and avoids the risk of puncturing.

5—4—3—2—1—GO!

As you acquire experience, so you will acquire your own techniques for dealing with the effort of time trialling. Try to begin concentrating on your ride and "visualizing" the effort before you start. Chatting in a relaxed manner to all and sundry immediately before the start is not recommended. One time triallist I know builds up a picture of a Formula One motor race start: he is in pole position, and must get away before the rest catch him.

You must try to build aggression, so that your adrenalin is rising before you start. Prepare yourself mentally for a painful first few minutes until you have reached cruising speed.

Start in the large chairing, with the chain on a sprocket in the middle of the block. Starting in a huge gear could strain your back. The "quarter to three" pedal position is recommended, as you are held in the starter's arms. Work your way steadily up through the gears, getting a good pedalling speed going in each one before entering the next, and then accelerating again.

Everyone has an optimum pedalling speed, dependent on background and morphology, although older riders tend to pedal more slowly, and younger riders more quickly. You will find yours naturally if you make sure that you can turn the pedals in a given gear, rather than fighting them. A cycle computer with a cadence counter function may help you establish this; 80 rpm is on the low side, 120 on the high side.

Most top time triallists have a perfect style that belies the effort they are making. There's a reason for this. If the pedals look as if they are turning on their

Jeannie Longo moves forward in the saddle to turn a big gear. Note the aero seat post, shoe covers and lightweight brake levers

own, it's because the body turning them is not being distracted by rolling head or shoulders or wobbling the bike to force an overlarge gear around.

WORK ON YOUR STYLE:

- Keep head and shoulders as steady as you can. Tri-bars will help here.
- Maintain one position in the saddle. If you can't keep comfortable for long, check your position before racing again.
- Try to concentrate on pulling up the pedals as well as pushing them down.
- If the gear you are in feels too big, change down. Then try to increase the revolutions gradually, using the muscles in your lower back.
- Pull with your arms against the pedal strokes — not too much or you will develop shoulder wobble.

MAINTAINING SPEED

Riders use a variety of mental tricks to maintain pedalling rhythm in a time trial. Listening to uplifting music with a good "pedalling beat" before the start can help, as it will then circulate in your mind as you pedal. Others continually count the pedal revolutions.

While most of your mind remains focused on turning the pedals, there are five sources of information that you should be constantly comparing: the pulse rate on your pulse monitor, the speed on your computer, the gear you are turning, the pedal revolutions and the pain in your legs. The object is to ride at the highest pulse rate within your pre-set limit in the highest gear you can turn comfortably. If you don't have a pulse monitor, you will have to judge your intensity from your breathing and "feel".

You should have some idea of the intensity you want to ride at, in terms of your pulse rate, from your training: work out the upper and lower pulse limits that you want to ride in before you start, and try to stick within them. You will probably find a natural pace is about 15 beats below your maximum. Try not to drop below the rate you wish to ride in, and at all costs do not go above it except on a hill followed

POSITIONING FOR OPTIMUM AERODYNAMICS

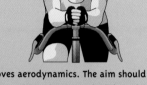

Frontal area can be reduced by bringing the elbows closer together, moving gradually from a position as that in the left-hand diagram to that on the right.

Lowering the head also improves aerodynamics. The aim should be to move gradually from the position shown on the left to that on the right.

Moving the position of the pelvis is vital in order to flatten the back for greater aerodynamics. The diagram on the left shows a rider who is forced to sit upright as if on a chair; the rider on the right has the pelvis turned. Like all position changes this takes time.

by a descent where you can recover.

Whatever, you must remain concentrated on YOUR ride: if you see the rider who has started a minute ahead, try to lift your pace to catch him, but stay within your limits. If you are caught, try to use the other rider as a marker, but again don't overcook it. Don't be afraid to change gear for any obstacle such as wind or a hill — keep in your optimum pedalling rate, and try to work out just how hard you can go. Try to start hills within yourself, then gain speed over the top, rather than flying at them and "blowing up". In the final mile, you can intensify your effort, allowing your pulse rate to drift over the limit you have set, so that you cross the line a few beats below your maximum pulse rate.

LONG DISTANCE
Seasoned time triallists will ride a 50-mile time trial at the same intensity as a "25", or just below, while less experienced riders are likely to find that if they attempt to go at "25" pace they will run out of steam at 35 or 40 miles. Thus, you should pace yourself slightly below the intensity at which you would ride a "25" — if you find you have energy left after a first attempt, increase the intensity slightly next time round, and so on until you find the optimum pace.

Bear in mind that you will have worked out your optimum short-distance pace after several attempts, so your first longer-distance events should be treated to some extent as experiments. Your short-distance training and racing should have given you the ability to ride at speed, so in the weeks leading up to your first "100", substitute one longer ride of four or five hours per week for one "level three" session — and allow yourself a day off to recover afterward.

You should not need to eat anything in a "50", but you will need to drink either water or a prepared glucose polymer drink such as Maxim or Hi5. The latter is probably a good idea, as you will eliminate any chance of running out of energy close to the finish. It's a good idea to experiment with various drinks while you are out training to work out which ones suit you best. A prepared energy drink is best because then you are taking on carbohydrate as well as liquid, and you will not run any risk of "getting the bonk".

A 100-mile time trial is a more serious proposition: most riders will only tackle one or two a year as a necessary qualifier for a club or regional Best All Rounder competition. The elite, clocking around or below the 3–40 mark, can ride them at the same speed that most riders would aim to achieve at 10 miles: for mere mortals the objective is to get round in a respectable time.

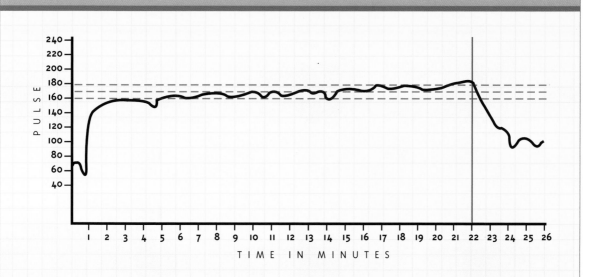

PULSE RATE DURING A 14KM TIME TRIAL

240
220
200
180
160
140
120
100
80
60
40

PULSE

1 2 3 4 5 6 7 8 9 10 11 12 13 14 15 16 17 18 19 20 21 22 23 24 25 26

TIME IN MINUTES

How a pulsemonitor graph might look for a 14-kilometre (eight mile) time trial. The rider starts after a minute, (hence the dip as he ends his warm-up), and the pulse rises rapidly to the anaerobic threshold, which is about the 165–170 beats per minute mark. Towards the end of the ride as the finish approaches it is well over threshold, it rises to the finish, then descends rapidly after the chequered flag. The two dips might be brief downhills.

Pacing has to be different for 100 miles. For novices doubling your time at "50" and adding 10–15 minutes would be realistic. The aim in a "100" is to ride at a rhythm you can sustain for the full duration, because starting fast and "blowing up" will result in a more serious loss of time than at 50 miles. You will find some kind of schedule — for example, splitting the race into 25-mile segments — helps, although you should be prepared to be flexible with it if the weather changes. Base your plans on the likely wind direction, and the nature of the terrain. The bad patch will come anywhere, although the consensus seems to be that between 65 and 80 miles is the most likely time. All you can do is keep your head, and resist the urge to panic. As the finish approaches you will get going again due to the psychological boost of knowing the end is near.

Many riders suffer unnecessarily in a "100" because they do not drink enough: you should aim for a bottle an hour as a minimum, and for a race of this duration, you must be certain your stomach can cope with what is in the bottle. What is an irritation in a "50" can be impossible in a "100". Experiment with different drinks on long winter training rides. Strictly speaking, if you have carbohydrate in the bottle, you don't need to eat, but it may

settle your stomach. See the section on eating in races in the previous chapter for more information.

In a "100" it is a good idea to persuade a friend or spouse to come along and hand up bottles — they can also give you an idea of your progress compared to clubmates/friends/rivals, and their presence will give you an additional motivation to keep going when it gets tough. If you have no helper, don't rely on getting round on two bottles — they won't be enough. Before the start, leave two bottles in a carrier bag at the 50-mile point, ideally where the marshal can see them, and stop for 30 seconds to pick them up — you will lose far more than this amount of time if you get dehydrated. If you are getting bottles handed up, vary the contents — you may find that pure water will sit most easily in your stomach at the later stages.

Note that for a "100" you should carry a spare inner tube or tubular and a pump, or make sure that your helper has spare wheels in the car, and is keeping a close eye on you — imagine getting to 90 miles and failing to finish because you puncture. If you are not aiming to win, a puncture will not be the end of the world and changing the tyre will only cost three or four minutes. At shorter distances you are not permitted to have

a car following you with assistance, due to the traffic problems it can cause. For a "100", it is permitted.

A 12- or 24-hour event is not to be taken lightly, and not to be tackled until you have completed several "100"s. Basically the same rules apply as for a "100", but more so — you must pay more attention to feeding, taking solid as well as liquid food, put in more long-steady-distance training beforehand, and maintain a pace that should not go high into level three for any sustained period.

HILL CLIMBS

As far removed from a 12- or 24-hour time trial as can be — you won't ride these at level two! The season for hill climbs — as their name suggests, brief time trials from bottom to top of a designated hill — is a short one, beginning in mid-September and ending in October with the National Championships, one of the most atmospheric events of the British cycling year.

Hill climbs vary from sprints of little over a minute up steep monsters to 15-minute slogs up the passes of the Dales and Dartmoor. Unless you discover you have a leaning for them and become a specialist, you may get no further than an annual club championship, which will

TAKING TURNS IN A FOUR-UP TEAM TIME TRIAL

The leading rider swings out, and decelerates down the line to slot in at the back

still be a fun exercise.

Two basic points apply: the lighter you and your bike are, the bigger an advantage you will have, while the training, which should come on top of a full season's racing, should be made to match the race. If it's a one-minute hill, base your training around one-minute to 90-second intervals at a near-maximal pace, while for a longer hill, do longer, more sustained intervals, where the pace should not be maximal until the very end.

Reconnoitre your hill well — if possible before the day itself, so that you can decide what gears to use. Short hill climbs are won and lost on your choice of gears. On the day, warm up well, continuing as close to your start as is possible. Arrange for someone to have clothing waiting at the top — and go!

HILLY TIME TRIALS

The short-distance time trial on a hilly circuit is becoming more and more popular in Britain as traffic forces races off "out and home" courses on main roads. Many riders like to ride these in the early season, but there is now virtually a year-round calendar, and there are several season-long series based on selected events nationally.

A slightly different approach is called for compared to an "out and home" event. Knowledge of the circuit is very important, particularly for the beginner — if you know how fast you can take a certain descent or how long a particular hill is, it is a vital psychological and tactical boost. And you must be aware of road junctions for safety reasons. So reconnoitre the course beforehand —

US Postal Service in team time trial action, with barely any space between the riders as they seek maximum shelter

ideally on the bike a couple of times in the weeks leading up to the race, and at the bare minimum in the car the day before. Make sure your bike has the gears you will need. On the day, the main ploy to remember is that you should not attack the hills at a workrate above that which you would usually employ — if you go "into the red" you may pay the price later. It's better to stick at a steady rhythm, based on your usual racing pulse rate, and pick up speed smoothly over the top. Only give it everything close to the finish. On descents try to pedal for as long as the gradient allows, rather than freewheeling automatically.

TEAM TIME TRIALS

These vary from the two-man (or "two-up", as the jargon has it) events that form many riders' introduction to the racing season in March, or their epilogue to the season in the autumn, to longer four-up events. The principle is the same: you are as strong as your weakest link.

Many road racers ride team time trials early in the year as a prelude to a full season's road racing, while — given that the intensity is similar to that of a mountain-bike race — off-road racers will not suffer from doing one or two either.

The same "shelter" principles apply as described in Chapter 8 on road racing, with the difference that for four-up team time trials, it may well be better to opt for a "one line" formation rather than the classic "two lines" of the road race break. The point of this is that each rider is able to make the pace for as long as they feel they can, allowing the stronger men to take more of the workload: in the "two-line" formation, the workload is shared equally, putting the weaker riders at a disadvantage.

It's crucial to train with your partner

or partners before the event — and one session is probably not enough — to work out where your respective strengths and weaknesses lie, and agree how you are going to take turns. Some teams agree that each man will do a certain number of pedal revolutions on the front — more in a tailwind, fewer in a head- or crosswind; others agree simply to play it by ear. It is vital not to compete among yourselves — it can be a good idea to appoint one experienced rider as "captain", to decide how long turns should be and what should be done if one rider punctures or blows up.

TRI-BARS

These aerodynamic handlebar extensions, which clip on to the handlebars, have become ubiquitous in time trials everywhere since Greg LeMond's dramatic victory in the 1989 Tour de France. By enabling the rider to adopt a lower position, frontal drag is reduced, and the lower back muscles can be used more efficiently.

If you have one bike that you use for training and racing, try to get a pair of tri-bars that will clip on under the bars, as this enables you to get a lower position. If you race a great deal, a hand-built frame to your specification will help — then you can investigate designs with a lowered front end, or a downward-sloping top tube, or a 26-inch front wheel, depending on what your builder advises. But don't rush into this — such machines are expensive, and you have to get them right. Better to evolve a position using road frame and tri-bars, then get a custom machine.

The tri-bar extensions should be fitted parallel to the ground or with a slight slope upward — up to about 15 degrees. They should not slope

David Millar is relaxed and comfortable as he gets down on the tri-bars

downward or steeply upward — a downward slope will affect handling, while an upward slope will be less comfortable. Adjust the fore and aft movement so you have the soft part of your arm a few inches in from the elbow resting on the pads, while your fingers can grip the turned-up ends.

Then you can think about up-and-down adjustment — this is done by moving the stem up or down, not pointing the bars down. Start with the bars as low as you can go while remaining comfortable, then over a period of months move them down by 5 millimetres at a time until they are as low as you can get them without impeding forward vision. This must be done progressively.

The eventual aim with tri-bars is to end up with the body parallel to the ground or even sloping forward slightly. This is not something that can be achieved quickly — it should be done over several months in conjunction with stretching exercises for the lower back and hamstrings. The humped position that is adopted by many cyclists when they ride on tri-bars can be eliminated by rotating the pelvis as per the diagram on page 70 — you will need several months' experience of riding with tri-bars before you begin to do this.

The frontal area can be reduced by narrowing the arms so that the air flows smoothly around the body and the arms do not act as a brake. Move the armrests closer together progressively so that the arms are almost touching.

Thirdly, the chin needs to be lowered so that the head does not protrude, but is tucked in. Again, you will need to do this progressively — aerodynamic positions such as Lance Armstrong's are not achieved overnight. Note that you must be able to see clearly ahead.

SAFETY

This issue has increasingly entered the spotlight in recent years due to the vast increase in traffic on our roads and has led to a move away from the use of main roads, particularly dual carriageways. The "low-key" nature of time trials means that many road users do not realize there is a cycle race taking place, so they are not prepared to encounter cyclists riding at speed. As well as the usual safety procedures you follow on your bike, the following tips should be noted:

- Wear a helmet that will protect you if you fall off. Note that smoothed-out aerodynamic headgear may not meet recommended safety standards. You should check before you buy so you know what you are getting.
- Do not ride with your head down: each season there are instances of riders hitting parked vehicles because they are focusing only on their effort.
- Do not "cut" corners. Cars may approach you from behind at speed.
- Pay particular attention, if riding on a dual carriageway, to the points where sliproads join and leave. These are where most accidents happen, as cars joining or leaving the carriageway simply do not see the cyclist.
- Do not slipstream other vehicles. This looks enticing but is dangerous and, not surprisingly, is against the rules.

TIME-TRIAL JARGON-BUSTING

Best All Rounder — competitions run at club, regional and national level for all age groups across various set distances from 10 and 25 miles for under-16s to 50 and 100 miles and 12 hours for men. The times/mileage for each distance are combined: quickest average wins. The most important is the British Best All Rounder, run by Cycling Time Trials, over 50 and 100 miles and 12 hours for men, and 25, 50 and 100 miles for women.

Dragstrip — a fast course, usually on a dual carriageway.

Gift hill — on some fast out and home courses, the regulations permit the inclusion of a hill that is descended at the start, but not climbed at the finish. Strange, but true.

Minute man — (or, in certain cases, two- five- or ten-minute man). Name usually given to the rider starting one minute ahead of you.

Scratchman — usually the fastest rider in a race: the man off last.

SPOCO — regional series based on placings in events on specified Sporting Courses, hence the acronym.

Sporting Course — the opposite of a dragstrip, where you will not have to contend with traffic, but your time may well be slower.

Two stars of cycling, two contrasting approaches to aerodynamics. Sean Kelly, above, has not managed to get his torso paralell to the ground, has his hands apart, tri-bars sloping upwards and his elbows close to the knees giving him the look of a man who only occasionally time trials. The specialist Chris Boardman, below, has his torso flat, enabling him to move slightly forward on the saddle, with hands together, elbows further forward with the tri-bars flat. The equipment chosen tells the same story: Boardman has an aerodynamic hat, seat-post and front wheel, together with an electric gear shifter to reduce weight

7: OFF-ROAD RACING

MUD, MUD, GLORIOUS MUD. WHETHER FAT TYRES OR THIN ARE YOUR THING, YOU'LL BE AMAZED HOW MOUNTAIN BIKING AND CYCLO-CROSS GET INTO YOUR BLOOD. SO HOW DO YOU GO ABOUT BUNNY-HOPPING, AND AVOID FACE PLANTS, WIPE-OUTS AND WHEEL SPIN, SO THAT YOU CAN WHIZZ DOWN THE MUDDY TRACK TO SUCCESS?

It is easy to see why off-road racing remains popular, even if the current trend appears to be away from pure racing towards fun events. Mountain biking is particularly accessible and uncomplicated, while cyclo-cross has made particular efforts in recent years to make young cyclists welcome. Newcomers are rarely faced with a complicated licensing system or required to be in a club before reaching the start line.

The nature of off-road sport is slightly different from other sides of cycle racing too. Mountain-bike events present an individual challenge, pitting riders against the terrain as much as against each other. Many competitors, well aware that they will most likely never be up with the race leaders, still derive great satisfaction just from finishing a challenging course, hence the shift in emphasis towards "enduro"-type events.

So the fact that anyone can join in and take up mountain biking is a definite plus in its favour. But that in itself won't make them good mountain bikers. To be successful it is necessary to train, as mountain biking is a physically demanding activity. Experienced road and cyclo-cross pro Adri Van Der Poel of Holland described cross-country racing as being "the toughest test in cycling. I would compare it to an individual time trial lasting over three hours."

The analogy with time trialling is an apt one. Aside from technical skills and physical conditioning, mountain-bike racing is about pacing yourself. To do well you have to learn to judge the effort that will be required to keep you going through the whole race. Much of the effort in a mountain-bike race is a solo one, and success depends on avoiding "blowing up" by making too big an effort early on.

Watching a race in progress, comparative unknowns often feature near the front of the field at the end of lap one. These shooting stars nearly always burn out before the halfway stage, just about the time when the experienced riders are beginning to pick up the pace in readiness for the decisive final laps.

TRAINING

Training for mountain-bike racing can be broadly divided into two sections: riding technique and physical conditioning. The two are, of course, interlinked. The more often you ride, the fitter you get and the more used you become to your bike and its capabilities. But you can also target each area individually and treat any improvement in the other as a welcome bonus.

TECHNIQUE

It's no accident that some of the best bike handlers in mountain biking have a background in skiing, BMX, cyclo-cross and moto-cross. In all four disciplines people often start young, learning early the valuable lesson that a good sense of timing and the ability to read rough terrain is often a far more valuable asset than brute strength.

Without wishing to sound too much like a Zen master, the key to great bike handling is to be one with your bike. Understand how it will react in a given situation and, with practice, you won't even think about the moves that let you progress as smoothly and as quickly as possible. Instead you will make them instinctively.

This takes practice, practice and more practice. But be warned: turn training into a chore and you will be less likely to

succeed. Try out a new manoeuvre two or three times in a session. If it doesn't come easy, move on to something else rather than allowing yourself to become frustrated. You can always come back to it next time.

SKILL BUILDING

For these first exercises, you won't even need to go off-road. They can be practised in a playground or a deserted car park, anywhere reasonably level that's quiet and away from traffic. Turn them into a game and they can be a lot of fun too.

The purpose of these exercises is to give you a feel for the bike and its controls, to allow you to learn to relax and feel comfortable on it and to experiment with the subtle weight shifts and changes in body position that are the key to good mountain biking.

Start out really slowly in an easy gear and begin to turn circles around your playground. Gradually make the circles tighter and tighter. Try it in the saddle and out of it. Once you have taken this as far as you can go, start again but this time cut figures of eight. Again, decrease the figure each time and try it in different positions around the bike, leaning your body one way and then the other, seeing what effect something as simple as sticking a knee out has on balance.

Now set out a rudimentary slalom course with whatever comes to hand and weave in and out as tightly as you can. Start with your markers fairly widely spaced and every few passes move them nearer and nearer.

In all three of these games, constantly

The downhiller at work: note the motorbike-style full-face helmet, full protective kit and goggles

experiment with your body position as you go along to see how the bike reacts. Also, lay off the brakes as much as possible in order to appreciate how much you can achieve by body shifts alone.

These moves may sound, and are, ridiculously simple but they give a feel for the bike that will prove invaluable off-road. As you play and experiment, you should gradually discover that the centre of activity on a mountain bike is very different from that on a road bike. On the road, your body weight is centred on the saddle and moves around it. On a mountain bike, it is centred on the bottom bracket and moves around that.

TRACK STANDS

Standing still, believe it or not, can also teach you a lot about body positioning. Start on a gentle gradient by beginning with the crank arms horizontal — which foot leads is a matter of personal preference and what feels most comfortable — and your body forward out of the saddle. Now turn the front wheel slightly up the incline and try and hold the bike stationary.

If your body position is right, you should be able to do this by applying light pressure on the leading pedal and the brakes to balance the bike's natural desire to roll backwards.

BUNNY HOPS

Jumping bikes looks very flash, but few top cross-country riders ever do it. Watch an elite rider like Nick Craig or Liam Killeen tackle an obstacle and they will prefer to keep pedalling and finesse their way over it by absorbing it with their body, drawing the bike up towards them as they pass over. The pros know that jumping is hard on equipment — every bike shop has at least one customer who regularly totals frames and wheels this way — and involves breaking the all-important rhythm they have set for the race.

But there are times when it's a useful skill. Hopping combines two separate actions, lifting the front and the rear wheel, in one fluid motion.

Front wheel lifts are important for getting over obstacles. Lift the front wheel over a log, for instance, then shift your body weight forward slightly and the rear wheel will usually follow over the obstacle.

But for a full bunny hop the best place to start is by learning to lift the rear wheel. Start with the crank arms horizontal to the ground, your legs flexed and your head over the bars. Roll along at a slow speed and then push your feet down, back and up as smoothly as you can. To execute the back part of this motion, you may find it easier to point your toes down at the ground. Don't hit the brakes when you practise this move — you are more likely to go over the bars.

Bunny-hopping is not just done to impress, it can save vital seconds as well

Once you can consistently lift the rear wheel, it is time to look at the front end. Start in the same position as the rear wheel lifts, but this time push down on the front tyre. Then quickly pull back up on the bars to get the front wheel in the air.

It's time to put it all together. As you roll along, drop into a crouch with bent knees and elbows and then jump the bike up, using the bar pull for the front end and the rear wheel lift simultaneously. Get the timing right and both wheels should part company with terra firma.

Landing will be much easier if you make full use of nature's own shock absorbers — your arms and legs — and always make sure your front wheel is pointing straight when you land. If it isn't, get ready to crash.

Once you have gained enough confidence, start to hop small, preferably not too solid, obstacles so you can perfect the timing and power required for each jump. You'll soon realize that you need to be as near to the obstacle as possible before starting to take off, and that there is no need to jump two feet into the air to clear a four-inch high shoebox.

Another critical factor is the speed of your approach. When the obstacle is first in sight, speed up by pedalling faster, then stop pedalling as you near it and get ready to make your move, secure in the knowledge that you have the momentum needed to clear the obstacle in your way.

BUILDING A RHYTHM

Develop a smooth pedalling technique. Learn to pedal the full circle and not just the downstroke. It isn't always possible to spin the pedals off-road but do it whenever you can as it is a more efficient way of transmitting power and it also helps to maintain momentum.

Anyone who has ever ridden down one side of a valley and up the other side will understand how important momentum is. Have it on your side and the following climb is relatively easy. Lose it and you can waste a lot of energy struggling to the top.

Gear choice is a critical factor here. Mountain bikes have lots of gears for a reason — to encourage you to keep spinning — so make full use of them to maintain a steady cadence for optimum momentum and traction. Always change down before any obstacle, corner or climb — it's better to spin over than grind to a halt.

THE VISION THING

Momentum and rhythm are extremely important and the key to maintaining them is anticipation. Adept riders read the trail a long way ahead rather than just seeing the next immediate move. Their body already knows what that is and reacts accordingly, allowing them to concentrate on forthcoming attractions.

Obviously, confidence in your own technical skills makes this easier to do. But learning to look at the whole picture from an early stage makes good sense. When you can scan from just in front of the bike to the furthest point on the trail that you can see you find that there is less need to slow down for obstacles. Gradually you discover that instead of lurching awkwardly from one problem to another you are travelling faster and more smoothly than before.

PICKING A LINE

Bikes tend to go where you are looking. If you are staring at that intimidatingly large rock protruding from the track ahead rather than the clear line to one side of it, the chances are that you will hit that rock and your worst nightmares will come true. Concentrate on where you want to go at all times.

BRAKING

Perception of danger prompts many beginners to apply the brakes when one of the paradoxes of mountain biking is that riders often have more control when they let go of the brakes and concentrate on picking a good line. This is because, on rough ground, less shock is transmitted through the bike at speed.

This isn't a licence to commit mayhem, however, but a recommendation to use the terrain to your advantage and work out the best time to brake.

Taking a corner, for instance, the time to brake is before the turn begins, where the traction will usually be better than on the bend itself, and then steer round it and accelerate out. If the outer edge of the bend is banked, there may be no need to brake at all. Simply lean the bike into the turn and follow the contour of the bank in much the same way as a track rider does in a velodrome.

Wherever you ride, try and avoid locking up the brakes. This leads to skidding, which is ecologically unsound, as well as causing you to lose momentum and control. Oh, and it wrecks your tyres. It's better to learn to scrub off speed by feathering the brakes, gently applying them alternately and together to slow progress but not stop it.

DESCENDING

The golden rule of downhilling is: keep your weight back. As the front wheel begins the descent, stand on the pedals and shift your butt back behind the saddle, flex your legs to absorb shocks and extend your arms without locking them at the elbows.

This position looks very gung-ho but it's the safest one to be in. With the body's weight positioned over the rear wheel there is reduced scope for being thrown over the bars. To maintain control, brake primarily with the rear brake, as the front one will automatically pitch the body forward. Never lock up the front brake — it could send you over the bars.

CLIMBING

Going uphill it is essential to maintain traction and control. The best way to do this is by learning to select the right gear for the hill and knowing when to stay seated and when to stand on the pedals while climbing.

It requires a certain amount of mental discipline to remain seated on a climb. The natural inclination is to stand up, but the seated position keeps body weight over the rear wheel, preventing it from spinning out and losing traction. The downside, however, is that it can unweight the front wheel, causing it to lose line. Leaning forward with the elbows flexed out counteracts this effect.

Unless the climb is really short or very rocky, try and start it in the saddle. You can always stand up from this position if the climb demands it. But if you start standing up, it is very difficult to drop back into the saddle without a loss of momentum.

Rising out of the saddle improves leverage, allowing you to pull on the bar-ends, and power. Since there is a risk of losing rear wheel traction, body weight has to be finely balanced between front and rear wheels, which can involve lots of minute but critical weight shifts during the course of the climb.

STRETCHING

Many people's memories of their first off-road ride are of the adrenalin rush of their first serious descent and the all-over soreness they felt the next day. Because your body takes a greater hammering off-road than on, the best way to minimize the risk of damaging muscles is by stretching before and after every ride.

Stretching isn't just about damage limitation, however, it is also about increased flexibility. A supple rider can spin the pedals more readily and can produce more power, simply because muscles are able to move more efficiently.

To be most effective, a pre-ride stretching session should be done when the blood is pumping and muscles have been warmed up, after five or ten minutes of easy pedalling. As with eating well, the effects are tangible. You will feel more limber and flexible on and off the bike if you stretch regularly. A full range of stretches for cyclists is included in Chapter 14.

WEIGHTS

Pulling on the bars to lift the front wheel off the ground, many beginners find themselves tugging harder with their dominant hand and, as a result, fail to land the front wheel in a straight line. This is logical enough — right-handed people are generally stronger on their right-hand side than their left and, for left-handers, vice versa — and it affects pros as well as first-timers. The former world champion Ned Overend, for instance, used to regularly take a series of tests at the sports clinic in his home town of Durango, Colorado, to make sure that his strength was balanced equally on both sides of his body.

Working with weights is the best way to cure this imbalance. It also has practical benefits in other areas too. Working on particular leg muscles, for instance, improves strength and power. Mountain biking demands greater upper body strength than road riding, so it is helpful to work on the arms, back and shoulders with weights to prepare them for the rigours of downhilling and climbing.

The object of weight training for mountain biking is not to look like Arnold Schwarzenegger but to be more efficient on the bike. The way to achieve this is by combining light weights and high repetitions for each exercise. Explain to the instructor at your gym what you are trying to achieve and he should advise you of a programme to suit your needs.

PHYSICAL CONDITIONING

Immediately after winning a silver medal at the 1995 World Senior Women's Downhill Championships, Mercedes Gonzalez of Spain (via California) said that she trained on the road 80 per cent of the time. There is a lesson to be learned here — methods of building fitness in one discipline can be applied to another.

Whenever you are training, your breathing and your body can tell some of the story of what is happening during the workout, but the information they provide is hardly scientific. A heart rate monitor is an invaluable, albeit expensive, tool for those who want to train seriously.

Any exercise will only work through repetition. Each component in this programme needs to be repeated at least three or four times to have any benefit. And each component is progressive, starting with a minimum recommended duration, so that as you get fitter you can extend the duration of the exercise.

The first thing a beginner needs to do is get the body used to being on a bike for any length of time. Keep things simple by starting out with road rides or undemanding trail rides of between 45–60 minutes' duration two or three times a week. Concentrate on keeping a steady cadence and maintaining a pace at which your breathing is regular and you are starting to sweat a little but not experiencing any muscular discomfort.

To more experienced riders this level of effort may sound familiar. It is in effect a "recovery" ride, one undertaken at 60–65 per cent of maximum pulse rate. If you are making the transition from regular road riding to mountain biking, you will want to do one or two of these rides per week and up the duration to 1.5–3 hours. But if you are a beginner you should start with shorter rides and gradually increase their duration over the course of several weeks or even months, depending on where you are starting from.

Once the body is accustomed to the effort it is time to up the workload a little. Again, do these rides once or twice a week on road or easy, relatively flat trails but this time maintain a brisk tempo. Start at one hour duration and work up to three hours over the course of a couple of months. On these rides, breathing is regular but deeper and you are more acutely aware of your muscles. This equates to what has been described in Chapter 4 as medium intensity.

These first two types of ride are what are called steady state rides, where the heart rate stays more or less constant, and they are the main elements in building an endurance base.

The next step is to shorter, more intensive sessions to improve the body's oxygen supply system. Begin at a steady pace and, once you are warmed up after 20 minutes or so, increase to high intensity, as if riding a 10-mile time trial on the road. The effort is really noticeable and it is much harder to keep your breathing regular. This is hard work: mentally you are already planning a rest day for tomorrow and are glad you only have to do this once a week.

Beginners won't be able to sustain this effort for long, only 5–10 minutes at a time. More experienced riders will be able to last longer, though it isn't recommended to keep going for more than half an hour. Vary the terrain you use for this exercise, hammering up hills one day and on the flat the next. This level of training is similar to that used for road time trialling.

Finally, maximum intensity intervals are short, repetition-based sessions that provide great aerobic conditioning. Once you have warmed up, go flat out, sprinting as hard as you can for 30 seconds. The effort should leave you gasping for breath and send your heart rate near or even over the anaerobic threshold. Allow five minutes to recover and then do it again. Repeat the effort eight to ten times, each time allowing five minutes to recover in between efforts. These sessions can be increased by 15-second increments as you grow used to the exertion required. But always listen to what your body is saying before

Thomas Frischknecht climbs, balancing his weight between front and rear wheels, using the arms for maximum leverage

Read my eyes: this downhiller is not just focussing on this corner, but is already lining up the next one

extending the duration of any session.

How these components fit together into an overall training schedule is determined by what you have as a goal. A commonly used pattern is to work on a basis of three weeks of hard training followed by a week of recovery riding and rest. By varying the components within the schedule, you can work on year-round fitness or train to peak for a particular event.

Whatever the goal, most coaches will emphasize the importance of steady state work and rest and recovery, because these provide a powerful fitness base and reduce the risks of overtraining.

RACING

So your entry has been accepted and it is time to get yourself, your kit and your bike ready for the big day. The key to success here, as with so many other things, is to plan ahead. That way, if something does go wrong, there will be enough time to put it right without panic. Otherwise, it may sound obvious but the principles of eating sensibly and sleeping well that are outlined elsewhere in this book apply equally to mountain biking as well as road racing.

More specifically, pre-riding the course if it is held on a circuit repeated several times is an essential part of your pre-race build-up, so that you can be aware of difficult sections and perhaps go over them several times. Look on your race entry details to see when practice sessions are being held. In enduro events, the course may be kept secret until the day — accept the element of surprise as part of the challenge.

Most races start early, as a full programme has to fit a variety of categories into its schedule. This usually means that practice is limited to the day before. If the venue is far from home, you may need to book accommodation or be prepared to camp overnight.

Once you have established when you plan to arrive at the race, the first thing to do is enlist a helper to accompany you. Going to a race by yourself is a lonely experience that is not recommended. Having a clubmate or family member

alongside you offers both practical and psychological advantages.

Helpers can calm pre-race nerves, hand you feed bottles, look after your kit and congratulate or commiserate when the race is all over. Since racing takes it out of you, you may also want them to drive you home.

Mountain biking is hard on equipment. You should be in the habit of cleaning and maintaining your bike on a regular basis — unless you like spending a fortune on repair bills. A thorough checkover is essential before racing. Do this five or six days in advance, so if anything is wrong you still have time to get down to the bike shop for spare parts and rectify the problem before you leave for the race.

Assemble the kit you intend taking with you. Apart from obvious items, such as cash or credit cards, a mobile phone and a watch, the starting point is to divide your baggage into four sections: bike and emergency spares; pre-race and practice kit; race kit; and post-race kit. Make checklists to ensure that you pack everything you need.

Bike and emergency spares will include: inner tubes; a tyre; a spare chain; a CO_2 cartridge or mini-pump and, if possible, a track pump; a chainbreaker; lubes and bike-cleaning kit, such as a bucket; brushes, rags and sponges; Allen keys and basic spanners; and a first-aid kit, including a few spare safety pins as race organizers never have enough of these for race numbers.

During the race, no outside technical assistance is allowed. Most riders carry a spare tube, usually part inflated, and a CO_2 cartridge or mini-pump, a 6mm Allen key and, often, a chainbreaker with them in a jersey pocket. Wrapping the tools in a rag will stop them rattling around.

Pre-race and training kit will include: a racing jersey and undervest; shorts and long tights; socks; shoes; a tracksuit top or fleece; a hat; a helmet; gloves; a waterproof jacket and trousers; a pen and notepad.

The race kit list duplicates many of these things, but don't skimp on the overlap. If the weather is foul or the circuit includes a stream crossing you will be glad to have a fresh set of dry kit for the race itself: a helmet; shoes; socks; a jersey; arm warmers; an undervest; shorts or tights; gloves; water bottles.

The riding kit in both cases includes items, such as arm-warmers or undervests, that you may not need if the weather is hot, but it is best to be prepared by always carrying them just in case.

After the race it is essential to get dry and warm as soon as possible, so you will need plastic bags for dirty clothes; a complete change of clothing; a carbohydrate energy drink and towels, flannels and a shower kit. Depending on conditions, sandals or wellington boots are useful too.

AT THE RACE

When you arrive the first thing to do is register at the race organizer's tent, where you will be issued with your race number and advised of the pre-race routine. Then go out and have a look at the course if you can do so.

Downhillers often walk the course, closely inspecting every section, then ride it. For cross-country riders, a ride around is usually enough but be prepared to stop to look more closely at the terrain. Some sections — such as climbs where you may need to choose between riding and carrying the bike — and extremely technical sections, you may want to tackle more than once.

What you are looking for are the best lines to take, which gears to select for each section, where potential problems may occur, where you may have to carry the bike and where you may be able to gain an advantage over your rivals. You may also want to change your tyres for particular surfaces. For downhillers and those with suspension bikes, adjustments may also need to be made to suspension settings, while tyre choice can be critical. Watch too for the feed zones, where your helper will be able to hand up your bottles during the race.

Taking notes during this course practice may help, as will visualizing what the course will be like during the race with other riders all around you. The goal is to be thoroughly prepared for the next day by building a mental map of the circuit, so the race itself will hold as few surprises for you as possible.

THE RACE ITSELF

Whether you are racing cross-country or downhill, starting from cold is not a good idea, so beforehand wrap up sensibly and go for a good warm-up ride — at least 20 minutes — to get the blood flowing.

A good start is important in cross-country racing and enduro events. Unfortunately, everyone else on the start line knows this, so the beginning of most races resembles a cattle market in bedlam.

Whatever happens, when the whistle is blown or the gun goes off, don't panic. The important thing is to settle as quickly as possible into a rhythm that you feel comfortable with. To a degree, this involves ignoring what is going on around you. If the race begins at a faster pace than you expected, don't be tempted to push too hard to keep up. All you will do is blow up, so it's much better to set your own level and stick with it. The principle involved is akin to that of time trialling on the road — ride hard but stay within your limits.

During the race you will overtake and be overtaken. The etiquette of overtaking is for the slower rider to give way if the track allows it. The polite way for an overtaking rider to warn a slower one of his presence is to shout "Track!" or "On your right!" The impolite way is to turn the air blue with abuse. Don't be ruffled either way. Just keep your pace steady.

Get the pacing right and, inevitably, you will soon begin to overtake those who have done too much too soon. What matters is how you feel, how well you have prepared your mental map so you know what comes next and how well you have prepared yourself so that your body can cope with this test. Get it wrong and you will suffer — but store up what you have learned for future reference. Get it right and you will finish tired but satisfied.

CYCLO-CROSS

There is increasing fusion between mountain biking and its older relative, cyclo-cross. In Britain, you can ride many local cyclo-cross races on your mountain bike, while many of the stars who race mountain bikes in summer turn their hands to cyclo-cross in winter, either as training or to rake in a little extra cash.

For a mountain-bike racer, the arguments for 'cross are convincing — the level of physical effort is similar, if slightly more intense; the courses are different, but the technical demands are

closely related. 'Cross is equally useful for the road-, time-trial or track-racer.

A major problem for summer racers is maintaining the intensity of training through the winter: it's easy to go out in a group and ride tempo, not so simple — mentally or physically, given restrictions such as weather, darkness etc. — to train at higher intensity. The attraction of cyclo-cross is that you get a very intense one-hour workout similar to a 25-mile time trial or a breakaway in a road race, but without having to try to do it on the road. No surprise, then, that a lot of top European road racers used to ride 'cross. Now they tend to go and train in Tenerife all winter, but that option is probably not open to you.

Cyclo-cross is accessible and easy to enter — you just turn up, pay and ride for all except a handful of major events. Entries for under-16s are free or reduced.

EQUIPMENT

You are allowed to ride many cyclo-crosses on your mountain bike, but there is a minor problem — the courses are designed for the lightweight specialized cyclo-cross bike, without the long climbs or lunatic descents of many mountain-bike circuits. You may have to carry your bike — and if a mountain bike gets clogged with mud, it will weigh a ton. The best thing is probably to experiment on a mountain bike if you have it, trying to make sure beforehand that at the very least you're not racing on the wettest courses. Wait until you're certain it is for you before investing in a specialized cyclo-cross machine such as that described in Chapter 2. If necessary, invest some time and a few phonecalls to local bike shops in adapting an existing road bike — preferably using a training frame rather than your best racing one — for 'cross; tyres, gear changers and pedals are the key areas if you're just dabbling.

RACE TACTICS

As in mountain biking, there are none. Get a good start and ride as fast as you can, at "time trial" pace — as fast as you can without blowing up. The start is essential, but, unlike mountain biking,

senior races are not split up into ability categories, so bear in mind that if you're a beginner, it's regarded as discourteous to take front row on the grid and get in the way of the serious racers.

As with mountain-bike racing, foreknowledge of the course is crucial. It's likely to include more obstacles such as run-ups, tricky climbs, descents and corners in a shorter circuit, so pre-riding the course several times is vital. Work out where you will have to change gear, and what gear you will change to, what line you should take out of corners, where you will have to dismount. Make sure that your tyres are not pumped up so hard that you are losing traction: can you let a bit of air out? Look for bits of mud that may churn up, and plot alternative lines. And it sounds basic, but make sure you know where the start and finish are.

Look for any bits of the course that suit your personal strength, be it climbing, running or descending. If you need to attack a rival — be it for 1st or 21st place — this will be the place to do it. Equally, be aware of the sections that you will find tougher. If you are involved in a man-to-man battle, make sure at least that you lead into the section. It will be harder for a rival to get away if he has to come round you rather than attack from in front.

You should aim to complete looking at the course with plenty of time in hand — enough at least to change into race clothing, wash any mud off the bike, and gulp down some carbohydrate drink while you gather your thoughts. When you come to warm up, ride for at least 15 minutes, including a little bit at race pace so your system is prepared. If there is a bit of road nearby, warm up on this, to avoid the risk of puncturing or clogging up the bike. As you will be racing in the cold, warm up in extra clothing, and hand it to a helper before you start.

TECHNIQUE
The key techniques to master in cyclo-cross are getting off the bike, carrying the bike, and getting back on again — you may have to do this many times in a race, so it is pointless being fit if you lose time here. Practice is the only way — do this off-road, but somewhere where you won't constantly be getting in the way of horse riders and walkers.

Dismounting at running pace sounds complex, but is easy in practice, thanks to the advent of mountain-bike clipless pedals. Swing your right leg over the saddle so that your thigh is between your left leg and the bike, grab the top tube two to three inches in front of the seatpin, and jump off, as you do so pulling your left foot out of the pedal and putting as much weight as you can through the right arm on to the top tube. Land on your right foot and start running, lifting the bike on to your shoulder as you do so.

There are several points that it is worth noting:

- Before you dismount, get in the gear you will need when you get back on the bike.
- If you are dismounting during a climb, do so while you still have momentum, or you will risk stopping altogether.
- If you are dismounting at speed, keep one hand close to a brake lever so you can adjust speed at the last moment if necessary.
- Dismount as close as you can to obstacles such as hurdles, ditches, etc., so you are off the bike for the shortest possible time.

Running with the bike sounds simple, but there are two ways of carrying the bike: taller riders pick the bike up by the top tube, flick the top tube on to the shoulder, then place their arm around the head tube and hold one brake lever. Shorter riders pick it up by the down tube, then place the crook of the elbow under the down tube with the hand on one drop of the bars. The crucial factor is that the weight of the bike should be well back behind the body — if it is forward, you will have to bend over, which makes it hard to see where you are going.

Remounting the bike is more straightforward. Hold the bars with the left hand and the top tube with the right to lift it off the shoulders. When the bike is on the ground — don't drop it too hard as you can lose control of it — jump on from behind, keeping both hands on the bars.

Practise getting your feet clipped in immediately — this is vital.

Climbing is a key area. As on a mountain bike, on slippery climbs keep your weight as far back as you can, for maximum rear-wheel traction, without lifting the front wheel. Don't move the bike as you would on the road, as it may slip. On shorter climbs, approach at full speed and try to power over in a big gear.

Descending needs the same technique as on the mountain bike: keep the body back, let the legs and arms act as shock absorbers, and keep hands on the brake levers. Don't hesitate to take one foot out of the pedal to use as a stabilizer on a corner or a cambered section. On flat, cambered sections, you will have to take the uphill foot out to stay upright.

Tree roots are a problem on wooded courses. Try to pull your front wheel up as you go over a root, as if it comes into contact with a muddy root you will fall off. Your back wheel will slide as well, so shift your weight forward slightly and try to flick it up.

TRAINING
In addition to the technique training described above, running is useful for the cyclo-cross rider, as you will have to run in almost every race at some point. Build up steadily from about 15 minutes to about 20–25 minutes, preferably on grass rather than tarmac, and stretch before and afterward. Make sure you have adequately padded shoes. If you are simply aiming to get some variety and intensity for the next road season, running and technique training, plus level-two sessions on the road, should suffice.

If you want to take it a bit more seriously, long off-road rides on the cyclo-cross bike are a good way of rediscovering your bike-handling skills after a summer on the road, but be sure that the route you choose is appropriate. As the winter progresses, switch to shorter sessions midweek concentrating on technique and high intensity, allowing plenty of time for rest. If you can find an area that is lit where you can train in the evenings both on tarmac and grass, that is ideal. Or try to find a local circuit on bridleways and back roads that takes about an hour, which can be done at near-race intensity before work.

8:ROAD RACING — BASIC SKILLS

LET'S ENTER A SMALL, MOBILE, GLAMOROUS AND VERY COMPETITIVE WORLD, WITH A LANGUAGE OF ITS OWN. WHERE SHOULD YOU SIT IN THE PELOTON, AND HOW DO YOU FORM AN ECHELON? HOW DO YOU CLIMB LIKE LANCE ARMSTRONG, CORNER LIKE LAURENT JALABERT AND DESCEND LIKE DAVID MILLAR? IT'S ALL HERE.

Road racing is not for the fainthearted. It requires a good degree of fitness and bike-handling skill merely to compete at entry level, but once bitten most participants are hooked by the exhilaration of riding in a bunch at speed, and the infinite tactical nuances.

One thing counts in road racing — getting across the line first; the rest is incidental. In this little mobile world where it's every man for himself, you need to learn which strengths you possess, and cultivate them to the full, and attempt to compensate for your weaknesses. All this will take time, and will need more commitment for less return than you may get from other branches of cycling. But if you succeed, the satisfaction will make the effort worthwhile.

Of all the branches of cycling, road racing is the most complex. Before you can think about winning races, there are certain techniques that must be acquired.

LEARNING TO RIDE IN A GROUP
The key skill required in road racing of any kind, from a local evening criterium to the Tour de France, is the ability to share a limited space of road with other cyclists in a close-packed group that may vary in size from two to 200 — the bunch, or in cycling slang, the "peloton".

Study television pictures taken from a helicopter of the Tour de France bunch as it speeds its way towards a stage finish and you will notice several things: the proximity of the riders' front and back wheels — rarely more than a few inches, or a few feet on a high-speed descent; the fact that the riders are effectively shoulder to shoulder; the constant movement in the peloton as riders move forward and slip back; the precise line followed by the whole bunch as it lines up and races through a corner.

Skill in riding in a bunch at speeds of up to 50 miles per hour is at least as important in road racing as pure physical ability. An experienced road racer who can anticipate the movements made by a group of riders and react accordingly, while remaining relaxed, will save energy and will be able to stay with a bunch longer than an inexperienced rider, even if he is not as strong physically.

The specific skills called upon for road racing are best practised in a small training group, and will be described later. But the basic skills required to ride in a group can be learned by taking part in group rides at lower speed, such as winter club runs. The great advantage of these rides is that there is not a lot at stake — in a summer road-race training session, riders are less likely to have time to pass on advice about how to ride in a group, and may be less tolerant of inexperienced newcomers who may endanger their safety.

The most useful skill you will learn from riding with others on a regular basis is getting used to the fact that other riders are no more than a few inches away alongside you, in front of you and behind you. Experienced riders will frequently rub shoulders by accident as they become involved in conversation — you don't have to learn how to do this, but you must get used to the idea that it may happen, and stay relaxed if it does.

Learning to maintain your cool with other riders around you is important for safety reasons. You are less likely to overreact, throw on the brakes, skid and bring down others when someone moves abruptly to avoid a pothole, for example.

- Ride with your front wheel a few inches to one side of the back wheel ahead, so if the rider ahead slows slightly for any reason, you won't come into contact with the wheel.
- Ride with your hands on the brake hoods rather than on the drops or the top of the bars — you have more control, particularly if someone comes into contact with your shoulder, and you can apply slight pressure to the brakes with your fingers if necessary. Always use the front brake, then the rear, and brake gently.
- Be aware of what is coming up ahead, so that you can anticipate the way the group will react to a corner, a pothole, a humpbacked bridge. If you are tall, you will be able to see over the riders ahead of you. If not, learn to look round them.
- Learn the art of "double-focusing". You should continually transfer your field of vision from the wheel of the rider ahead to the front of the group and beyond.
- When on the front of the group, be prepared to signal possible dangers ahead, particularly potholes, parked cars and cars approaching in the opposite direction. "On the left", or "On the right", or just "Left" or "Right" are the usual calls, often accompanied by a hand signal.
- If a vehicle approaches from behind, the rider at the back of the group will issue a warning, usually the word "oil". When in the group, be ready to act on such signals: they are common practice in road race bunches as well as on club runs and are vital for everyone's safety.
- Avoid sudden actions such as braking sharply, moving backwards as you stand up to ride out of the saddle, or jinking to left and right. Try to ride predictably.

This road-race peloton is spread across the road as it tackles a climb at a steady pace

On steady group rides, by watching and emulating the more experienced riders around you, you will learn how a group functions as it corners, tackles a climb, or rides through a crosswind, and you will learn how to anticipate the movements of the other riders. But it's even better to practise these skills in a group moving at somewhere near road-racing speed.

Frequently, road racers from a club or area train together in midweek evenings in late spring and summer: "chain gangs", as these informal sessions are known, are a good way to get used to coping with riding in company at race speed. The same ground rules apply as for riding in a group anywhere, with the added proviso that it is all taking place at higher speed.

You may find that "chain gang" sessions are too tough – typically, the group will be small, and it will move at the speed of a break in a road race, and may be equally competitive. Be prepared to look and learn for a few miles before peeling off.

Given the skills called upon in road racing, it is probably unwise to start a road race until you have gained experience in riding in a group. You will find it easier to cope, and you are less likely to endanger the other riders.

RIDING IN A BUNCH
While the same ground rules apply for riding in a road-race bunch as for riding in any group of cyclists, there are several important differences: there are more of you, you are moving more quickly, and you are using the whole of one side of the road, or – in windy conditions – the whole road. Except on closed circuits, in Britain there will be traffic coming against you.

Generally speaking, a bunch rides in one of three formations. A bunch in single or at most double file will be moving at high speed, during a spell when riders are trying to escape from the front, and other riders are trying to follow them, or during a period when a group of riders on the front are working together to pull back a breakaway group, or approaching the finish.

As the riders at the front of a bunch relax and slow down after a spell of attacking or chasing, the riders behind them will not slow down quite as quickly, but will move alongside the riders who have just been making the pace, causing the whole bunch to fan out across the road. A bunch filling the road from one side to the other is one where no one is particularly willing to make the pace.

In a bunch moving at speed, stay as close as possible to the wheel in front for maximum shelter, and keep your front wheel a little to the left or right of the wheel ahead. Which side depends on the wind direction – if it's coming from your left, your wheel should be slightly to the right of the wheel ahead, and vice versa. When the bunch is lined out, be particularly attentive for possible dangers ahead – a parked car, a pothole. Usually warnings will be yelled out, but other riders may have their heads down too.

If you want to move up to a better position when the bunch is lined out, try to be clever. Use the slipstream of another rider who is moving up so that you save energy. Wait for a slight lull and use your momentum, going down the sheltered side if it's possible.

In a fanned-out bunch on open roads, you have to pay particular attention to oncoming traffic, as the chances are some riders will encroach onto the other side of the road. As they move back into the carriageway when a car approaches, jostling may occur. Also beware of the "concertina effect" caused by braking at the front. Crashes are as common, if less spectacular, at low speed as they are at high speed.

If you're tired, and you're at the

back, try to take advantage of any let-up to sneak forward — everybody else will probably have the same idea, but what you must do is react quickly and grab a good position when someone attacks and the bunch lines out again.

Unless you're completely worn out and hanging on for grim death, the front half of the bunch is the place to be. If you want to take a serious part in the race, you should be in the front quarter, ready to react if a dangerous split occurs, and sizing up the other riders alongside you while you consider when to make a move. Even if you are playing a waiting game, being at the front will enable you to observe your rivals, as that is where most of the riders who are taking the race seriously will be found.

Even if you don't feel strong enough to break away, near to the front you're less likely to get caught in a crash and you will have more time to react to any accelerations due to attacks. This is a key way of saving energy because as the bunch accelerates you can slowly build your speed, rather than suddenly having to sprint.

The golden rule is to hold the line when the pace goes up, even if you're tired. If you back off, expecting someone else to increase the pace for you, the bunch may split in front of you, and you will then have to bridge the gap yourself, losing valuable energy in the process.

BEGINNING TO RACE
The best introduction to road racing can be gained at one of the off-road circuits around the country. Here you can get used to racing in a bunch without the distraction of oncoming traffic, and as you can enter on the day, you do not have to go through the formalities of entering in advance. Your club will be able to advise you about the nearest venue.

On the day, make sure the bike is in perfect working order — this sounds obvious, but a surprising number of cyclists find last-minute glitches — arrive in plenty of time so there is no panic before the start, warm up well and relax. If you are riding on an off-road circuit and you cannot hold the pace, pedal round until the bunch catches you up and rejoin. You cannot compete, but you can at least gain more experience.

Packing close: riding in a road race bunch is about learning to share space, and thinking of your fellows

GIMME SHELTER
All road-racing tactics are born of one key principle: the fact that when one rider shelters behind another, he uses up to 25 per cent less energy than the rider leading. Therefore, as a general rule, two riders sharing the pace will ride more quickly than one, three will ride more quickly than two, and so on.

However, the "shelter principle" also means that it is possible to ride through a whole road race hidden in the bunch, saving your energy for one effort in the final five kilometres or the final 500 metres, tactics used to excellent effect by the great sprinters such as Mario Cipollini, and rather less impressively by most riders of lesser ability.

The ramifications of these two principles give road-racing tactics endless subtlety. If a group of energetic riders can escape the bunch and cooperate, while most of those behind prefer to save their energy, one of them will win. On the other hand, if the numerically superior bunch can be persuaded it is in their interests to cooperate against the breakaways, the attempt to escape is doomed to failure.

If you aren't planning to sit in and wait for the bunch sprint, a road race becomes a series of split-second decisions depending on your physical feelings, the course, and the competition: whether to attempt to break away or split the field; whether to go with a break as it forms; whether to try to get a chase going behind a break. For an experienced, motivated rider in good form, such decisions make themselves almost instinctively: if you are a road-race novice, it becomes your task to gain the necessary experience and find the fitness.

SHARING THE PACE
So what does a group that is sharing the pace together look like? Two parallel single files of riders will be visible: one line of riders is moving forward to take their turn in making the pace at the front of the line before swinging to their left or right. They will swing out to whichever side the wind is coming from, even if there is only a light breeze. Then they drop back, down the side of the forward-

moving file, until they reach the end of the line and swing across to begin moving forwards again. Why do they move out into the wind? So that as they drop back, they are giving shelter to the faster moving cyclists coming up the line.

A group of riders working in this way will maintain a high speed as they each move through to take their turn before easing back. This, typically, is how a breakaway group functions, and how some or all of a bunch chasing a break will cooperate. Study a video of any Tour de France stage and you will see this happening as riders attempt to break away, and the team that is trying to control the race tries to reel them back.

A breakaway group doing "bit and bit" or "through and off", as this is known, has its own rules: the speed has to be kept constant by each rider — not too low, so that momentum is maintained, but not too high, so that the rider behind is not sprinting to maintain contact. If the last rider in the line moving forward is courteous, he will yell "Last man" as he passes the next rider slipping back, so that he will have time to accelerate on to the back of the string. Particular attention has to be paid to the wind: if the road swings and the wind direction changes, the riders will move back down the other side. Getting the side wrong disrupts the group's progress and annoys your fellow cyclists.

If a rider has to take a break from working, to eat, or simply to get a breather, he will sit a bike-length or so off the back, still in the shelter, and yell "In" as the last rider comes down the group each time. Otherwise, the last rider will

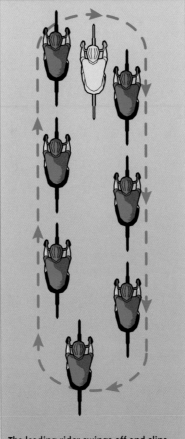

THROUGH & OFF

The leading rider swings off and slips back down the line to take his place at the rear.

think that he is going to accelerate forward to take his place, and the rhythm of the group will be broken.

In a break, try to position yourself so that you are behind the biggest man in the group — you'll get more shelter. If you are the biggest, follow a rider who's coming through steadily. If you are behind someone who accelerates strongly each time he takes his turn, you will be continually sprinting for his wheel and will use more energy than your fellow cyclists.

RIDING IN THE WIND

The third formation you will see a bunch form is the "echelon", which develops when the wind is blowing from the side. In calm conditions, or in a headwind, the greatest shelter is gained by sitting directly behind the rider in front. In a sidewind the most sheltered position is alongside the rider in front of you, with your front wheel lined up somewhere between his front forks and bottom bracket, depending on the angle of the wind.

In a crosswind, the whole line of riders at the front of the bunch will position themselves in this way, using the whole road. Then, if they are doing "through and off", the rider on the windward side will slip back, moving down behind the rest until he is behind the leeward rider.

Any riders who are not in the echelon are using more energy, which means that half a dozen strong men can easily split a race apart in a crosswind by starting an echelon, and cooperating well together.

Behind the echelon, one of two things will happen. Ideally, a second echelon will form immediately behind the first, and will go at the same speed until a more sheltered bit of road is reached. If the riders behind do not cooperate, however, they are condemned to a line-out "in the gutter", immediately behind the leeward rider in the echelon. They will use more energy, but may be able to hang on.

Riding "in the gutter" condemns many of the less fit riders in a race to being dropped, due to the extra effort necessary to fight the wind without shelter. When a race is lined out "in the gutter", it is crucial to be as close to the front as possible, so that riders are less likely to "sit up" in front of you and leave a gap that you will have to cross on your own. Even near the front, it is vital to keep an eye on the riders ahead — this situation on an exposed course will frequently see a split occur.

Echelons using the whole road occur even on open roads in Britain. In this case,

The rider in pink (right) has "swung off", and the rider in blue is "coming through"

RIDING IN THE WIND: MOVING UP AND FORMING AN ECHELON

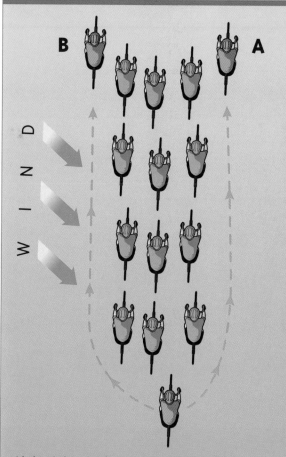

With the wind coming from the left, rider A has chosen to move up the sheltered side of the bunch, while rider B will waste energy as he moves up the windward side.

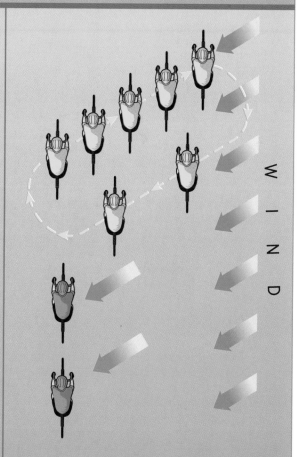

The echelon: riders move across the road towards the wind, then slip back across. The riders in green are "in the gutter" — they are getting the full force of the wind, and must get back into the echelon or lose contact.

Echelons: three distinct groups are visible on a windy day in the Tour of Spain, with riders "in the gutter" in between them

CORNERING

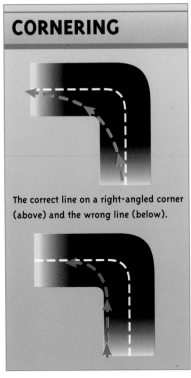

The correct line on a right-angled corner (above) and the wrong line (below).

Cedric Vasseur pedals through a corner with inside knee up and eyes fixed on the road ahead

it becomes even more important for rider safety to keep an eye out for oncoming traffic and parked cars, and to signal with the hands and voice.

CORNERING

Good cornering technique can win you races — and bad cornering can lose them. This is particularly true of criteriums in a city centre or races on short, closed circuits — during a one-hour city centre race on a one-mile circuit with four corners, you might have to sprint in and out of 100 corners — but it applies to a lesser extent on the open road as well.

- Follow the line of the other riders. If you are cornering in the middle of the bunch rather than in a single file you have no option anyway. Taking a different line can be dangerous.
- Brake before the corner — it's better to go in a little too slowly, than lose momentum and control by braking as you turn. Braking on the corner will make it harder to maintain control of the bike.
- Turn the handlebars as little as possible — try to turn by leaning into the corner. This takes practice.
- Take the straightest possible line through the corner, moving out to the centre of the road beforehand, cutting into the apex, and moving out to the

centre of the road again.
- If you can't pedal through the corner, hold the inside pedal up and the outside pedal down.
- For extra stability on the rear wheel, press your bottom into the saddle, and lean a little weight on the outside pedal if you can't pedal.
- Keep your head up. There may be another corner immediately, in which case you need to see what line the riders ahead of you are taking.
- Get an experienced rider to teach you cornering. Find a quiet circuit — maybe an industrial estate — and go round it on his wheel a few times.

CLIMBING

Climbs are usually key points in a road race. Because you are going more slowly than on the flat, the "shelter" principle is less important. A rider who is less fit, or simply heavier, will always suffer when the road goes uphill.

Longer, more gradual climbs are best tackled seated in the saddle, with your hands either in the centre of the bars, or on the brake hoods. The latter position is recommended as it enables your lungs to open more widely, and also means that, if you have brake lever gear changers, you can change gear without losing any momentum.

Shorter, steeper climbs can be taken

standing up on the pedals, using your arms to pull the bars up as you push the pedals down. This style gives you more power, but by bringing the arm muscles into play you tire more quickly, so it should be kept in reserve unless you are confident that you can get over the climb. Try to start the climb in the saddle using a low gear, then change up and go out of the saddle to respond to an acceleration, or to push your way over the top.

CLIMBING TIPS

- Try to maintain a constant pace on a long climb, going around slower riders, or dropping back a couple of places if necessary. If no one is attacking, concentrate on deep breathing and try to relax. Try to keep your shoulders still. Move forward slightly on the saddle and use your arms more when the pressure is on.
- If it is a particularly hilly area, try to reconnoitre the climbs before the race. Knowing you will only have to suffer around one more corner, or that the gradient is about to ease, is a vital advantage.
- Use a low gear — probably lower than you would use if you were on your own. This will enable you to flick around riders who have blown and are dropping back from the front.
- Always start a climb in the first third of the

bunch — otherwise you will waste energy working your way through riders who are dropping back. If you are a poor climber, try to start in the first 15. Then you can slip back slightly if the pressure goes on, and move up again if it is relaxed.

- If the bunch splits over the top of a climb, stay with the riders at the front, or join up with them, at all costs. What looks like a tiny gap on a hill can quickly become a large one.
- Look ahead, and change down before you need to if the gradient steepens. And if there is a tight bend, try to take the outside line — the gradient won't be quite as steep.

WHAT IF YOU CAN'T CLIMB...?

- The best way to improve your climbing is to lose weight — from your own body as well as the bike. The bigger you are, the more important this is.
- Try to find flat races — finish a few of these, and you might well have increased your power, and your ability to follow wheels, enough to get through a hillier one. If you can get through a 40- or 50-mile flat race, you will do your morale and fitness more good than by getting to 15 or 20 miles in a hilly race then blowing up and struggling on your own.
- Tour de France champion Lance Armstrong improved his climbing by losing weight, and also by long training camps in the mountains. A week in the mountains of Southern Spain, or the Alps, will bring you on if you're looking to develop the specific muscles that you need for longer, sustained climbs. Training in this terrain will also give you level three and four workouts without much mental effort. Equally, a couple of weeks riding the big hills in the Yorkshire Dales or the West Country moors will improve your confidence.

DESCENDING

Breaks can be made on descents, but they are also useful for defensive riding — for getting across to a group that has attacked over the top of a climb, or for getting back on to the bunch if you have got left behind on a hill.

Position on the bike while descending is important. If the road is bumpy, or twisting, use the drops of the handlebars and sit slightly further back, to keep a low centre of gravity, compensating for the fact that you will be hitting bumps at up to 50 miles per hour, and you are more vulnerable to the wind. Try to keep your weight more on the back wheel than the front, as the more weight there is on your front wheel, the harder it will be to keep your bike under control.

On long, straight sections, for maximum speed, put the hands close to the stem in the middle of the bars, and try to get your torso as low as possible, with your knees as tight in to the top tube as possible, and the pedals in a "quarter to three" position. In addition to making you more aerodynamic, this will allow you to absorb road shock through your bent legs.

- Use your body as a brake. To lose speed slightly, you can raise your torso from horizontal to an angle of 45 degrees, which increases your drag. Or, on corners, push your inside knee out.
- In a bunch, keep your distance. Particularly in less experienced fields, allow yourself more distance to react to the riders around you. Where you might aim to be six inches to a foot behind the rider in front on the flat, aim for at least a bike length on a fast descent. The faster the descent, the further apart you will end up.
- Go with the flow. The more relaxed you are, while remaining alert, the better you will descend. It's even more important than usual to "read" the road and the riders ahead of you due to the high speeds you will reach.
- Brake before the corners. This rule applies on the flat, but is even more important downhill because of the increased speed. You can brake more, for safety's sake, as you will accelerate more quickly out of the corners.
- Don't snatch. Squeeze the brakes gently, using the front first, then the back. You will use the front brake more. Don't jab the brakes suddenly, as you will lose stability.

Don't try this at home: a Spanish pro gets as low as possible on a downhill. Only for the confident — or foolhardy

9: **ROAD RACING ADVANCED SKILLS**

YOU'VE MASTERED THE BASICS. NOW YOU CAN START TO THINK ABOUT GETTING TO THE FINISH LINE FIRST. WHETHER YOU WANT TO SPRINT, WORK IN A TEAM, RIDE A STAGE RACE, GET BACK TO THE FIELD AFTER A CRASH, OR WORK ON YOUR WEAKNESSES, IT'S HERE, PLUS, HOW TO LAUNCH THAT ALL-IMPORTANT RACE-WINNING ATTACK.

The old adage about learning to walk before you can run is utterly appropriate where road racing is concerned — due to the tactical complexities inherent in sharing the road with 60 other riders, you need to acquire the basic skills outlined in Chapter 8 before you can think of winning road races. Mere strength is not always enough — you must know how, where and when to use it. Here is a brief guide to some of the tactical niceties that give road racing its enduring fascination.

BREAKING AWAY

Waiting for the bunch sprint is not always a reliable tactic. Even if you are a talented sprinter, at some point you will have to try to get away from the bunch, either to form a break, or to join one that is forming, without bringing the entire field with you.

Never attack from first place in the line: all the riders behind have to do to stay with you is to follow your acceleration. Instead, slip back a few places and aim to go past the riders on the front several miles per hour faster than they are travelling, and a few feet to the side of them. Then they will have to accelerate more suddenly and will have at the very least to make a bigger effort to close the gap that you will have opened. When the bunch is lined out in a crosswind, attack on the opposite side of the road — making sure no traffic is coming — then switch back. Anyone wanting to get on your wheel will have to make an unpleasant effort in the wind.

Keep going for at least half a minute before you look round and see what has happened. If the bunch are still there, watch out for anyone using their momentum to counter, then relax and

move back into the group to recover.

If you're on your own with a gap, try to settle into "time trial" pace, without going into oxygen debt, and ride along on your own — unless you're close to the finish, in which case you just have to throw caution to the wind and go for it. If other riders are coming across the gap, don't slow too much, but let them make the effort to catch you.

If you turn round and there are other riders with you, try to start doing "through and off" in two lines in order to build a gap. Get over a minute clear of the bunch and you can afford to settle into a rhythm, but during the period when you're trying to gain that time you will all have to ride close to maximum intensity. If the others can't or won't cooperate, you may have to accept that this break is going nowhere. Better, attack again, and see who comes with you.

GOOD PLACES TO BREAK AWAY:
- Over the top of a hill. Attack at the bottom and the bunch may be able to keep you dangling for the whole hill, and you may not have enough energy to keep away over the top. Make your effort just before the summit while the bunch is still in a line, ideally just as the road begins to level out; the riders on the front of the bunch may be unwilling to respond after climbing up the hill. A hill with a bit of level road before the descent is ideal for this.
- As a break is caught. The riders in the break are tired. The riders at the front of the bunch have been making an effort, and may think that if the first break has come back, so will yours.
- From a break as another group comes up. If it's near enough to the finish to risk it on your own. The members of your group will assume the riders coming up

from behind will catch you. They, in turn, may assume that when they have caught the rest of the group, that is it.
- In a stretch of crosswind. Unless you are really strong, only try this if the road changes direction soon and you get some tailwind. Calculate how long you can last in the crosswind on your own. Try to pass wide of the group, on the windward side, so that to get to your wheel, the rider on the front will have to move into the wind.
- Breaking away into a headwind on your own is not recommended — but if a group of you can get away before the headwind and work well through it, you will make big inroads on the bunch, none of whom will want to ride in the headwind.
- Where you can't be seen. Narrow, twisting roads with high hedges, where the race will line out as riders fight to stay at the front, are a better place to make a break than open, straight roads where you can be seen by the whole bunch.
- As the sprinters look at each other. Sometimes a race seems preordained as a bunch finish, and with a couple of miles to go, the sprinters begin gathering at the front. None of them will want to make an effort to pull a break back, so try to sneak away.
- When the bunch is feeding. Bunches tend to do things together, and this includes drinking and pulling things to eat out of pockets during a natural lull. Before they can catch you, they'll have to stop chewing.
- After a *prime* (see p109). The effort of sprinting for a prime will frequently draw a few riders clear. Either attack from the bunch as it catches them, or pretend to go for the prime and keep going.
- After a crash. As the other guys look

back, get up the road. At worst, those who have fallen will have to lose energy getting back on.

- As the rain starts. Morale droops, you escape, and then the bunch has to go fast on nasty wet roads to get you back.

THE SPRINT FINISH

Unless you are significantly stronger than the rest, and have good time-trialling ability that enables you to win regularly on your own, you will need to learn the art of sprinting, man to man or woman to woman.

The "shelter principle" is key in a sprint, because the speeds involved are much greater than normal. Gauging your effort is vital: go too early and you will blow up; go too late and you will cross the line cursing. You should bear in mind your reserves and aim to cross the line totally spent — it is the finish, after all.

Sprinting from a break is more straightforward than taking on a whole bunch. As you near the finish, you should look at the other riders who are with you and try to assess which will be the biggest threat: are there any you know by reputation? Is there one who has been regularly missing turns, but looks fresh? Who looks the strongest? Who has been sprinting for primes?

It does no harm to make a little effort — not quite an all-out attack — on the final hill, just to see who responds most quickly. If you're lucky, you may eliminate one or two of the opposition. In any event, you should aim to stay on the wheel of one of your danger men until you make your final effort.

Usually during races in Britain you will pass through the finish several times, so study it carefully each time you do so. Don't leave it until the last lap: you may be occupied in chasing down an attack, or trying to break away. The key factors are the wind direction, and whether the road goes uphill or not. Even a slight drag, with any noticeable wind, will make the finish harder. Ride on the front to see where the wind is coming from. If the finish is not on the circuit, it is vital to go and look at it before the start. Knowing the precise location is crucial — 200-metres-to-go flags cannot be relied on, and by then it may be too late. Landmarks such as trees, telegraph poles etc. can help.

Try to work out where you will make your effort, and what gear you will need. If you have brake lever shifters, you don't need to start the sprint in your "terminal velocity" gear.

Unless you are confident that you are the strongest, and can crack the other riders with a long sprint, an uphill or headwind sprint has to be ridden from behind, staying in the shelter of the first rank of riders in the break until you know you can get to the line without blowing up. Be prepared to follow when the rider ahead makes his effort, but don't come past until you know you can get there. Surprising numbers of riders weaken in the final metres of uphill and/or headwind finishes.

A tailwind sprint has to be ridden from in front, as the "shelter principle" is less important. You can afford to go for a long sprint as you can go more quickly

Alessandro Petacchi, centre, "throws" his bike at the line and gets a little air, with his head down to observe the wheels behind

ATTACKING IN A CROSSWIND

The rider in yellow has broken away down the sheltered side of the bunch, several places back from the front.

road, you have to keep an eye on both sides of you for riders trying to come past. Go in one of the two gutters, ideally the most sheltered one — you only have to look one way.

- The kick. You can gain a yard of extra speed that can win you races by sitting down as you approach the line, and throwing your weight back at precisely the right moment so that the bike is pushed forward.

- Get practice. No two sprints are the same, so the more sprints you do, the better you will be able to cope with different circumstances. Even if you're going for 20th place, you can still learn from sprinting. And when you're out cycling with your clubmates, the odd sprint for a sign can do no harm, road conditions permitting.

- Against a faster or stronger opponent or opponents you have to make sure you get the type of sprint you want. Go for a sneaky late attack or a really long sprint if you're the slowest rider. If you're tired, but know you're faster over a short distance, cling to the wheel like glue and look for a short, late sprint.

- Don't imitate the pros. Among seasoned sprinters in the big races, all sorts of shenanigans go on in the final kilometres, particularly before a bunch sprint. They are pros. You are not. Don't try switching, hand-offs, pulling jerseys, or holding another rider back with your elbows. At best, such manoeuvres will actually slow you down. At worst, you won't be sprinting again for some time.

- Never give up. The finishing order is decided on the finish line, so that's when you should stop sprinting. This sounds obvious, but particularly in an uphill sprint a lot of riders will slow down in the final 50 metres. If you keep going, what looks like ninth place can become second or third, if not first.

THE BUNCH SPRINT

When the race finishes in a large bunch rather than a small break, the same basic rules apply as outlined above when it comes to making your final effort. The difference is in the run-up to the finish.

Energy saving is what matters in a bunch sprint. The greats of bunch sprinting, such as Mario Cipollini or Alessandro Petacchi, will never be seen at the front. You may not have a team to

without blowing up — it's a lot harder to pull back a length or two at 60 kilometres per hour than at 40 kilometres per hour, so it is vital to take the initiative.

- Use your arms. Always start your sprint out of the saddle, using your arms, for maximum acceleration. If you can develop the art of getting to a high speed, sitting down for a moment without losing velocity, then making a second effort out of the saddle, it can be devastating.

- Get your jump in first. Having calculated beforehand when you are going to go,

have confidence in your ability and do it, even if it means moving before anyone else. The couple of lengths you should gain if you go from behind will work to your advantage — as long as you have calculated correctly.

- Use the wind. If the wind is blowing from the side, try to come past the leading rider on the sheltered side as you make your effort. Then hug the gutter so that no one can come inside you in the shelter.

- Use one side of the road. If you make your final effort in the middle of the

THE BUNCH SPRINT

1: LEAD-UP TO THE FINAL SPRINT

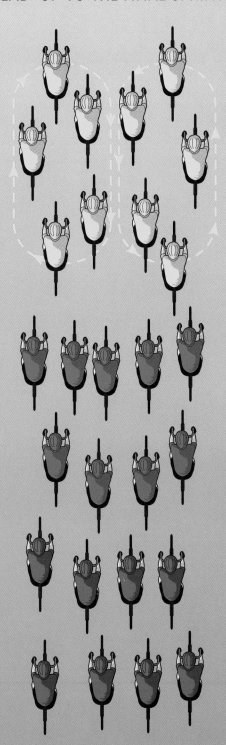

Leading up to the sprint the riders in green are in the ideal position — in the immediate shelter of the riders in yellow, who are making the pace. The riders in red are too far back.

2: INTO THE FINAL KILOMETRE

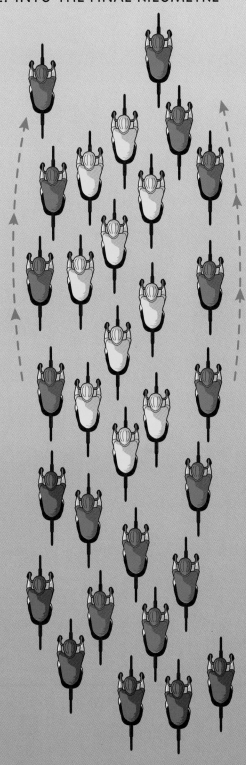

As the yellows and the greens surge forwards in the final kilometre, the red riders at the back get trapped as the leaders fall back.

TWO-MAN SPRINT

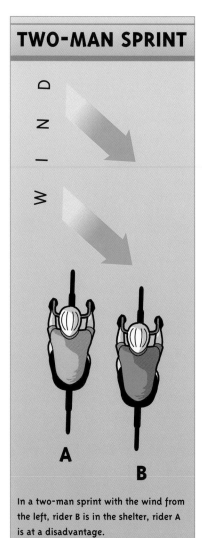

W I N D

A   **B**

In a two-man sprint with the wind from the left, rider B is in the shelter, rider A is at a disadvantage.

Breaking away: Nicole Cooke of Wales and Great Britain gives it everything, with no looking back

help you, as they do, but as the finish approaches, try to hold a place in the first 15 of the bunch — or in the final couple of kilometres of a tailwind sprint, the first seven or eight.

Then try to work your way forward. If you have to move up the outside, try to use the wheel of another rider so you don't have to make such a big effort. Inside the bunch, wait for gaps to open in front of you, then move in without thinking twice. Get on the wheel of someone you know is strong — if you know they are a good sprinter, that helps; if you can't spot someone with a reputation, get behind someone who has been racing strongly.

When riders start making their moves in the final kilometre, make sure

you hold your place. Fall behind here, and there is no way back — you will never make up the distance lost. Keep a cool head, and try to relax as the adrenalin builds. Be aware that riders who have been at the front, but do not have the strength or nerve for the sprint, will be dropping back at a far slower pace than the one you are travelling at. You have to get round them, without endangering yourself.

The "never give up" principle applies here as much as in sprinting from a smaller group. Riders will always drop back in the final 100 metres, as they lose their bottle or blow, even if it's flat.

If you can find a clubmate to help you out by giving you shelter until you make your final effort, and perhaps

"taking the wind" for you as you move forward, that will give you a considerable advantage.

If a threatening break goes in the final kilometres, you may have to race proactively rather than sit there and hope someone else does the work to bring the race together for the sprint.

If you are feeling strong enough to make two efforts, a cunning tactic if a group gets a few hundred metres ahead is the "false attack", in which you escape the field, and sit halfway between break and bunch for a short while. Chances are the bunch will ride up to you, then keep going to bring the break back. If you simply sit on the front of the bunch and pull, your rivals will rightly rely on you to do all the work.

TEAM TACTICS

A group of experienced riders from the same team who are all on form can control a road race, but only if they are well coordinated, and are prepared to sacrifice their interests for those of the team on a given day. The knowledge that on another day they will benefit from team support should be sufficient incentive.

At the lower levels of racing, team tactics are barely relevant, because teams rarely have any strength in depth. However, it is important to recognize what team tactics may come into play: if you are racing as an individual, you need to know what you are up against, and how you can profit from other teams' tactics.

- Blocking. A rider is up the road in a break. When the bunch start trying to ride "through and off" to chase the break down, one or more of his teammates disrupt their rhythm, by getting in the chain of riders and refusing to come through, or by slowing down as they come through. When a chasing group goes, one of his teammates will chase it down — either with the bunch on their wheel so that the chasing group will give up, or alone.

Then he will refuse to participate in the chase, getting a free ride to the front while he saves his energy.
- How you benefit: make sure you get away with riders who will have teammates blocking in the bunch. The chances of the break succeeding will be higher.
- Chasing. If a break goes without a rider from a strong team, or if their rider in the break punctures or blows up, the team will have to chase the break down by riding "through and off" on the front of the bunch, probably saving one or two stronger elements for later.
- How you benefit: if you're in the bunch, make sure you're at the front in case the chase causes a split. If you're in the break and you are told it is being chased down, try to get clear before it is caught. Then you may be caught by counterattackers.
- The old one-two. Two or three teammates in a lead group or a bunch will attack in succession, on the assumption that eventually the other riders will tire, and they will take at most one or two riders from the group with them.
- How you benefit: gamble on the right attack if you are alone. If you have teammates of your own, take it in turn

to mark each attack.
- Leading out the sprint. One or more teammates will ensure the fastest sprinter in the team has shelter right to the moment he wants to start the sprint. Alternatively, if there are two riders from the same team in a break, they may agree that one will go for an attack close to the finish while the other one tries to block any chase behind, and goes for the sprint if he is caught.
- How you benefit: If someone is getting a lead-out, try to take his wheel, then pre-empt him, or come past. In the second scenario, try to second-guess the two teammates and go with the rider who is going for a long one. Better still, attack before he does.

TRAINING FOR ROAD RACING

Paradoxically, the best form of training for road racing is road racing. Actually being in a bunch is about the only sure-fire way to pick up the bike-handling skills you need in road racing, while you also need to learn to read the way a bunch behaves and adapt your body to

Team tactics in action: five pink-clad riders from Spain's ONCE team mass at the front of the bunch to keep the pace high

the changes in speed demanded by a road race.

This is why top road professionals have to race during the build-up to a major target, even if they are merely treating some events as training — the "feel" of the bunch and the extra speed demanded cannot be replicated on your own for practice.

A winter spent building up your endurance and basic strength through level one and level two rides will provide a base on which to do the intensity work necessary before you start a season of road racing, but you can't merely train and then expect to win an event, unless you are very experienced and utterly confident.

With road racing, what you have to do is prepare as best you can, to a level where you can stay comfortably with a long club run, and where you can hang in with the local chain gang. Then you should start racing, and assess which areas you need to build upon.

To improve at road racing you have to increase the amount of power you can put out before you go into oxygen debt. This means interval training: long intervals to improve your ability to ride at a sustained level just below your maximum, and short intervals to get your anaerobic threshold up.

To improve in races at your level, once you have gained confidence, try riding harder events — longer races in a higher category. Start in the knowledge

that you are using such a race as preparation — essentially as a long ride at level two with spells of level three — and don't do anything foolish, like blowing all your strength on an early attack. Expect to be far more tired at the finish than you would be after a race in your usual category, and rest up for a couple of days. You should find that the greater speed, and/or distance have done you good.

STAGE RACING

If you are capable of finishing a one-day road race in a reasonable state, why not try one of the two- or three-day stage events that are to be found across the country at bank holidays?

Typically they include a time trial, and one or two road-race stages. The feel of racing for two or three days is completely different — camaraderie builds up between riders who are sharing the same roads for more than the usual Sunday morning. If you can get a team together from your club, that just adds to the fun.

Stage racing needs a little more organization than your usual Sunday morning jaunt (see Chapter 12 — The Start Line) and you need to prepare with a little more forethought. Take it easy for a couple of days beforehand — it's better to ride yourself in during the first stage than to turn up tired.

The overload principle applies here as

well — but so does the progressive bit! The weekend before, you could race both days, just to get get your body used to the idea, if it doesn't involve too much travelling. But unless the distances are longer, or the route is significantly hillier than you are used to, you can't really train specifically for the road stages.

Where you can make a difference, however, is in the time trial, which is usually included in a short stage race. It's a chance to gain time that cannot safely be ignored. So if your stage race includes a time trial and you fancy your chances, get in some time-trial training in the weeks leading up to it, if possible over the same distance and terrain that you will be racing over. You will have to use tri-bars, and will need to make sure that your body is accustomed to the different position.

During a short stage race of this kind, get plenty of sleep and stock up with carbohydrate before and after each stage — probably best in the form of one of the carbohydrate drinks on the market. If the stages are longer than you are used to, eat slightly more during the stages than you would usually do.

The tactics are fairly simple in a short stage race in Britain of the kind you are most likely to ride: finish as near the front as you can on all of the road stages, and lose as little time as possible in the time trial. Usually, team tactics matter less than physical strength — clearly, you should have an idea before the start of who the men to watch are, and you should keep this in your head during all the road stages. Alarm bells should ring if any of them get away.

TROUBLESHOOTING — CRASHES AND PUNCTURES

Punctures will happen no matter how good your tyres are. The first priority is to make sure that you don't cause a crash in the bunch. Keep control of the bike, lift one hand in the air to signal that you are in trouble — you should keep a weather eye open for this signal from other riders all the time in any race — and slip to the side of the road.

Many British road races do not have service vehicles with spare wheels. If your race has one, keep your arm in the air, try to signal to the car whether you require a front or a back wheel, and get the change done with the minimum of fuss. If you need a back wheel, before you stop,

Don't panic: This pro keeps a cool head — and a little distance — as his wheel is changed

Roll with it: Viatcheslav Ekimov of Russia comes a cropper on the cobbles in the Paris–Roubaix Classic, to no ill-effect

change on to the smallest sprocket. Then wait for the car to come up to the back of the bunch, rather than slipping back to it.

DON'T PANIC. Help the mechanic, but don't get in his way; he's probably better at wheel changes than you are.

A civilized service car may well attempt to assist you in getting back to the bunch by enabling you to take shelter: if this is the case, take full advantage until you are back in the line of vehicles behind the race. If not, you will have to time trial, or hope that a teammate is waiting to assist you.

In a stage race, you and your teammates should agree on what is to be done in the event of a puncture to one of your number — i.e. whether you should wait and assist him back to the bunch or not. If one of you is the race leader, several of you should wait and pace him back to the bunch as quickly as possible. The accepted drill here is that one, two, or even three of you should wait at intervals between the man who has punctured and the bunch — don't all go back and wait! When he catches up, he should be allowed to fly past the waiting rider, who gets in his slipstream, and gets used to the pace for a few seconds before taking his turn. Then it's "bit and bit" back to the bunch.

Crashes are something that will also happen no matter what steps you take to avoid them — at some point someone will fall off in front of you. Hard-shell helmets

and the clipless quick-release pedal have, however, taken some of the pain away.

If you learn to read the road and the way a group behaves, you are unlikely to crash, but there are certain precautions you can take:

- Learn to watch out for "cowboys" — the usual term for riders who are not at one with their bikes. Watch them as you would watch a bad driver on a motorway. If someone rides erratically, or persistently takes a dangerous line on the corners, try to keep in front of him or her.
- Watch for riders who are taking a drink — sometimes they will ease up and slip back.
- If someone slips a gear and you come up behind them at speed, don't panic. Use your hand on their backside to push them forward — you will decelerate, they will regain momentum, and you will have earned a friend.
- Be prepared for: humpback bridges; oncoming cars; riders who have punctured and are dropping back, arm in the air; potholes and gravel; speed bumps and traffic islands.
- If you fall, try to roll to absorb the impact rather than stretching an arm out to protect yourself. Better a torn jersey and a cut back than a broken collarbone. Get out of the road and on to the verge to assess the damage as

quickly as possible. And if you can, bring your bike with you.

ROAD-RACE JARGON-BUSTING

Much road-racing jargon derives from French, the lingua franca of the sport. Not surprisingly, it is often obscure to the newcomer.

Commissaire — official in charge of the safe and ethical running of a race.

Criterium — a town centre race on a small circuit.

Echelon — staggered formation adopted when riders are in a crosswind.

Neutralized — frequently road races start some distance from the changing rooms. Usually the field rolls to the start behind an official car, while a red chequered flag is shown. In this period racing is not allowed — the race is neutralized. A race may also be neutralized while it is going on, if there is an accident or the road is blocked for some reason.

Peloton (in English: bunch) — the main group in any road race.

Prime — a prize awarded during the race for the first rider past a given point. May be a hill prime, or on the finish line. Usually marked by a white flag.

10: TRACK RACING

FAST, FURIOUS, AND FRIGHTENING AT FIRST SIGHT, THAT'S THE WORLD OF THE BANKED VELODROME. BUT ONCE YOU'VE FOUND A TRACK, MASTERED THOSE BANKINGS AND LEARNED TO DEAL WITH A FIXED WHEEL GEAR, A WHOLE RANGE OF SKILLS AND OLYMPIC SPORTS WILL OPEN UP IN FRONT OF YOU.

Racing on a banked velodrome has much to offer — speed, excitement, variety, plus the fact that there is no traffic to worry about as there is when competing on the open road. Locally, track racing in Britain is run on a league basis, most offering a variety of events in an evening — usually midweek — for most categories. This makes this side of the sport ideal for beginners of all ages. With three or four races in an evening you get good value for your time and money, and you have more chances in a single session to gain racing experience than, for example, in a road race, a mountain-bike race or a time trial.

Road-racing novices in particular will find learning to ride the track beneficial. You acquire the same group riding skills, and the same ability to handle changes in speed that you will need on the road, but without the traffic you have on the open road, or the tight corners that characterize many road-racing circuits that are closed to traffic. In addition, if you find the pace too hard, you have the chance to race again and continue the learning process within an hour, rather than having to wait several days or a week for your next road race.

Track racing becomes addictive for many reasons. It's relaxed and informal. The variety of different competitions on offer prevents you from getting stale, and gives you more opportunity to find an event that suits you. Your helpers (and perhaps your family) actually get to watch you race all the time, rather than just glimpsing an occasional view from afar. As a spectacle, the sheer speed and elegance of a compact bunch pedalling in close formation is hard to beat. If you live near Manchester or Newport in South Wales, the indoor tracks at the British and Welsh National Cycling Centres enable you to ignore the weather.

The skills learned on the track transfer well into all the other branches of the sport. The pedalling speed acquired on the track will help a racer in any discipline to spin quickly and smoothly, expending the minimum of energy when the pressure is on, while the bike-handling skills that can be picked up — the ability to "rub shoulders" in the bunch, follow closely on a wheel, and to gain general confidence and speed up reaction times — are invaluable in road racing.

Many top road racers, particularly Australians such as the Tour de France stage winner Brad McGee, originally started out racing on the track, while others — of whom Chris Boardman is the outstanding example — have combined track racing with road and time trials to great effect. Many local racers take part in all three disciplines.

That doesn't exclude off-roaders either: the current rising star of British track racing, Jamie Staff, came to the track comparatively late in his career after taking world titles in BMX. It's never too late to take up track racing: 1995 British points race champion Jonny Clay was into his thirties and a successful road professional when he took the title. Proof positive that if you have a background of road racing, you can take to the track with relative ease.

THE TRACK FOR BEGINNERS
There are two factors that set track racing apart from conventional riding on the road: you have the bankings to contend with, and you will be riding a fixed wheel rather than gears as you will be used to on the road. See Chapter 2 for more details on track equipment.

First, those bankings. They aren't as bad as they look. Because most British tracks are large, and outdoors, their bankings tend to be innocuously shallow, compared to the steep slopes seen on the tight, 200-metre circuits used for six-day races in continental cities such as Ghent. The National Cycle Centre in Manchester is one of the steepest tracks used regularly for racing at 45 degrees, while the norm is between 12 and 15 degrees.

The key thing is to familiarize yourself with the idea that you can swoop up and down these slopes, and indeed use their downward slope to gain speed as you accelerate out of them. Fortunately, most tracks in Britain that offer regular evening racing during the week also offer beginners the opportunity to get used to riding the track in a non-competitive situation, using either their own road bikes, or track bikes that belong to the track and are hired or loaned to beginners.

The best way to begin track riding is through some of these "introductory" sessions, before graduating to training at "drop-in" or "open training sessions", which take place all year round at some tracks, notably Manchester. When you feel confident that you are relaxed on the track riding fixed wheel with no brakes in the company of other riders you should be ready to begin racing.

You will feel more confident on the bankings — whether training or racing — if you have done some group riding already, and are used to the idea of how a group of cyclists functions. Riding on the track in a bunch calls for more precision and concentration than on the road as

The ultimate in bike racing skill: track sprinters at a standstill, in essence a game of nerves to force the opponent to take the lead

riders tend to leave smaller gaps between wheels. This is because you are racing without brakes, so decelerating is a gradual process. You don't want to have to learn basic group riding and the art of riding the track at the same time, so it's best to get some group riding experience in first, as described in the first part of Chapter 8. Then you can concentrate on acquiring the quick reactions necessary for a fast-moving track bunch.

It's also important to get the hang of riding fixed wheel. This can be done on the road, although you should note that, unlike on the track, where you are not permitted to ride with brakes, on the road you must have a front brake. The fact that your legs control how quickly the back wheel turns means that the fixed wheel is itself considered as a back brake for legal purposes.

The best way to familiarize yourself with "fixed" is to put one on your road bike. You will need a track hub to do this, but a reasonable high-pressure rim with a track rear hub to train on won't break the bank.

On the road most riders opt for a gear somewhere in the 42x17 or 18 area. This is, of course, a much lower gear than you will use when racing or training on the track, where a gear between 51x16 and 47x14 would be typical.

If you already have several years'

regular riding on the road under your belt, it should not take too long to get used to the feel of fixed wheel, but if you are a relative beginner on the road it may take longer. The most disconcerting thing about "fixed" is that every now and then you will try to freewheel instinctively as you are used to do on gears, only to find your legs coming up at you in a disconcerting manner. Be prepared to relax your legs when this happens — if you panic and tense up you will flip upward in an awkward and perhaps dangerous manner.

In the years before derailleur gears became the norm, all cyclists would spend the entire season training and racing time trials "on fixed". You will find that in the less hilly parts of the country it is possible to do most of your winter riding on a fixed gear, if you so wish, with a consequent improvement in the fluidity of your pedalling. The other "plus" with the fixed gear is that there are fewer moving parts to pick up muck from winter roads.

You will soon appreciate the feeling of being at one with the bike and learn to "brake" through applying reverse pressure with your legs to slow down the pedals. Like any other change on the bike, take things steadily and be careful that you do not injure yourself through pedalling too quickly downhill or in too

big a gear up a steep hill before you are ready for it.

Although many tracks have bikes available for beginners to hire, and some offer "drop in and ride" sessions for riders who want to use road bikes to get the "feel" of the track, you will eventually need a second bike if you're going to race track regularly. Fortunately, the outlay is not great, because — as explained in Chapter 2 — the track bike is essentially a simple machine. To compete at over-16 level, you also need to be a British Cycling (BC) member, and hold a racing licence, which can also be used for road- and mountain-bike racing.

The main limiting factor where track racing is concerned is whether there is a track in your area. See the BC website **www.britishcycling.org.uk** for details, or contact BC at the National Cycling Centre, telephone 0870 871 2000.

THE TRACK LEAGUE

The local summer evening track league is where you will do the bulk of your track racing, although if you end up taking it more seriously, you will find that during the summer there are regular weekend meetings spread around the country, while racing on the covered velodromes continues all through the winter.

Most track leagues offer racing

A packed track centre at a six-day race in Germany, where a variety of track skills are essential

streamed into two groups, which may be combined for certain events. Usually juniors can race with over-18s in either group, while under-16 racing will also be on offer. In most cases, riders are competing for a season-long award towards which most of the events on a given evening will count.

Most of the events you will find are listed below: because track leagues are intended to be accessible, all are eminently reasonable targets for road racers, being bunched races or short-distance time trials. Riders who specialize in time trials or mountain-bike races will find it takes a little more time to acquire the necessary bike-handling skills.

TRACK TRICKS

Unlike time trials and road races, most track leagues are contested by a relatively small core of regular riders. If you wish to race with success, you have to make it your business to watch the riders you race with — if you can discover their particular strengths, weaknesses and the tactics they tend to employ, you will stand a better chance of success.

Another factor is knowledge of the track itself: they all have their peculiarities, and the better you know how to handle a crack in the concrete here and a wobble in the banking there, the more cards you will have in your hand.

When riding in "the string", as a single file of riders is called, you will be expected to put in your share of work on the front to maintain the pace — after your spell, which should last half a lap to a full lap, move up the track, allow the riders behind to pass below you, then slot in on the back, or into a gap in the string. This is something you will quickly learn at non-competitive training sessions.

When making an attack from a group on the track, the same principles apply as on the road, except that you will usually be looking to come past the front of the group at speed in a diagonal direction using the downward slope at the end of one of the bankings to give you greater acceleration. As on the road, an attacking effort has to be made from several places back in the bunch.

Because track league events tend to be short, the warm-up is crucial. Aim to spend at least a little time at racing intensity before each event you ride, so that the pace does not come as a shock to

the system. It may not be possible at an evening track league to spend much time on the track warming up while other events take place, so if you have a turbo trainer or set of rollers, take them along and use them to get the legs turning.

Take plenty of clothing, because you will be getting hot racing, then cooling down waiting for your next event, and outdoor tracks are not the warmest of places. Put on clothing immediately your race finishes, and take spare undervests so you can put on a new one after each event — ideally you should also change shorts and jersey if possible. Freshen up with a cloth and some cologne or sports wash as well.

DISTANCE RACES

Usually called "scratch" or "bunch" races, these are run on entirely the same "all start together, first past the post wins" principle as a road race. Distances are up to 10 miles or 20 kilometres, but at many track leagues they are run over five or eight kilometres, or 12–32 laps (depending on track size), to provide the maximum number of races during an evening. Some events may have a staggered handicapped start according to ability.

Tactically, you have several options. The first is to attempt to make a break a good distance from the finish, when riders waiting for the final sprint will be unwilling to commit themselves. This is a good idea for the proficient time triallist or road racer, who can take advantage of his stamina from the road.

The second is the do-or-die effort with around two or three laps to go. This is the only option if you are a non-sprinter. This has to be a total effort.

The third option is the bunch sprint — these tend to be much tighter than on the road. As in road racing the key is to stay near the front without actually doing any work, and then to avoid the riders who inevitably fall back as the sprint is launched.

POINTS RACE

Here you sprint every few laps for points down to third or fourth place, with double points awarded for the final sprint. Winner is the rider who has accumulated most points during the race, not necessarily the first man across the line. Instead of or as well as points, cash prizes

may be awarded for each sprint in which case the event is referred to in the French expression *course des primes* — a "prime" is a small cash prize, so this is literally a "primes race".

You have two options: stay in the bunch and sprint every few laps for points or attempt to gain a lap on the bunch. A lap gain effectively cancels out any points the other riders may have gained, until they regain the lap.

The "stay there and sprint" option is fine if you are a good sprinter, and particularly good if you have teammates to help you control any breakaways and give you the occasional lead out. Until you have gained some experience, base your tactics around anyone you know is a strong sprinter — watch what they do, where they place themselves in the bunch and how early they begin their effort. If you are not a strong sprinter, you will have to rely on attacking with between a lap and a lap and a half to go, as the sprinters are preparing to make their efforts.

The attacking option is a good one, as in the course of attempting to gain a lap you are likely to take points along the way — if you do, the effort will not have been wasted even if you can't get the lap. A good time to make the break is as the leading riders ease after one of the sprints — either attack as they drift back, or follow their wheels as they sprint, then use the impetus to get away. Keep your eyes open for potentially advantageous breaks — if you can get away in a small group, so much the better.

DEVIL-TAKE-THE-HINDMOST

Perhaps the most entertaining of all track events, where on each lap the last rider across the line is eliminated until the final sprint is contested by the last two riders on the track. If you are a good sprinter, you can hang back, and pick off the slower riders close to the line, but apart from that there are few tactics — stay close to the front!

TEAM PURSUIT

Two teams of four riders start half a lap apart and "pursue" each other around the track, usually for four kilometres. Both are timed, fastest wins — or may catch the slower if it is a small track and there is a big discrepancy in ability.

Technique relies on the road racer's

"through and off" (see Chapter 8), but is tighter — typically riders will do half-lap turns before swinging off, up the banking and back down to find the last wheel in the string. With the timing taken on the third man across the line, teams may nominate a rider who will give his all before peeling off with a couple of laps to go.

In the team pursuit technique and cohesion count for as much as the pure speed of each of the individual team members: if one rider cannot hold the pace, or one individual is too strong for the rest, the team's chances of success are greatly reduced.

OTHER TRACK DISCIPLINES

As well as the ones you will generally find on offer at your usual track league, there are other track disciplines that feature in weekend meetings and at national and world championship level.

INDIVIDUAL PURSUIT

The principles are the same as the team pursuit, but with two single riders on each side of the track. The initial field is whittled down through qualifying rounds to a final cut who fight it out man-to-man on a knockout basis. Distance is usually 4,000 metres.

At national and world championship level, pursuiters tend to be specialists. Road professionals such as Bradley McGee of Australia and the 2003 world champion Bradley Wiggins of West London combine the two but have to devote some time before the world championships or Olympics to dedicated pursuit training after months riding the road.

Any rider who has shown talent at short-distance time trialling can be considered to have a fair chance of success at the pursuit at local level. The basic training is essentially the same, but high intensity work has to be geared towards a more intense five-minute effort rather than a 20-minute one as in a 10-mile time trial.

The key areas that need to be worked on on the track are the standing start, where a novice, however strong, can lose

Great Britain's team pursuiters in action: the rider lying above the other three has completed his turn and will latch on to the back of the string

RIDING IN A TEAM PURSUIT

Pursuit teams doing half-lap turns: the leading rider swings up and drops back on each banking.

valuable time to a more experienced rider, and the technique of riding smoothly and quickly along the bottom of the track — any deviation from the shortest line equals time lost. Another basic factor that has to be looked at is communication from helpers on the trackside, who have to keep the rider informed of his progress.

Finally, as in all time trials, equipment and aerodynamic position become crucial at any level, so these should be looked at closely before you attempt a pursuit. You may benefit from stretching yourself out a little more on the bike, dropping the bars slightly for better air penetration, or fitting disc wheel and/or tri-spokes.

Pursuiting requires a cool head — if you are a slow starter up against someone who is quick out of the blocks you have to remain relaxed and aim to get your opponent when he weakens. Alternatively, if you are a fast starter, you can use this to good advantage to demoralize your opponent.

SPRINT

The most dramatic cycling discipline, a simple man-to-man speed contest. A series of elimination rounds, usually beginning with a 200 metres flying start time trial, is used to sort out the fastest riders who then compete in a knockout contest that should leave the two speediest men on the track.

Sprinting is the most specialized of track disciplines: building the high proportion of fast-twitch muscles needed to accelerate to 40 miles per hour and sustain the speed to the line requires a considerable amount of strength training, much of which is done in the gym — top sprinters are usually men with huge thigh and bicep muscles.

The specialized training and techniques required cannot be covered in the space available in this book — the relative paucity of world-class sprinters today is explained by the fact that, together with mountain-bike down-hillers, they are the only pure specialists in cycling and widespread career opportunities are not there for them as they are on or off the road.

Usually, sprinters cross over with the kilometre time trial — or the 500m for women, the "keirin", and a recently introduced event, the Olympic sprint, in which a three-man team is timed over three laps, each rider leading for a lap. The kilometre and Olympic sprint are currently something of a British speciality, so there are considerable opportunities for those who show early talent.

MADISON

Another spectacular discipline, fought out by teams of two over a set time. The winners are the team that covers the greatest distance — the object thus becomes for each team to lap the field whenever possible. If two teams finish "on the same lap", they are separated by the points they have scored at intermediate sprints and at the finish.

The twist is that only one member of the team races at a given time: his companion slowly circles the track — usually up on the banking above the racing — until it is his turn to take over. The changeover occurs when he is "relayed" into action by his partner, who usually grabs his outstretched arm and literally "slings" him forward to gain speed. The length of time between changeovers is optional.

The technical demands of madison racing are great: not only must changes be achieved safely and with the minimum loss of rhythm, but also riders must have a good awareness of what all the other racers on the track are up to, whether they are resting or racing, and anticipate what they are going to do. And there is the need to calculate the right moments to attack for a lap gain while keeping abreast of the overall race situation.

Experienced road racers who can also ride the track tend to be good at this, but the technical demands mean this is not a race for the beginner.

TIME TRIAL

Over either one kilometre or 500 metres, with either standing or flying start, this event is one that riders who have shown some aptitude for sprinting should seriously consider taking up, although it demands a degree of endurance as well as pure power.

The track time trial looks at first sight like a test of simple speed, but over a kilometre, an effort of just over a minute, it is rather more than that. A high level of self-knowledge is necessary to ensure that you keep enough energy for the final lap, when many riders "die" after making their effort too early. Britain's 2000 Olympic champion Jason Queally has said that the effort he puts in can be so intense that he coughs up blood afterward.

KEIRIN

Another specialized event, this Japanese import is one for the experienced sprinter and confident bike handler. Six or eight riders line up behind a small motorbike, which paces them until 3–500 metres to go, when they sprint it out. The jockeying for position that goes on before the finish sprint and the final spectacular battle means this is not for those of a nervous disposition.

MOTORPACED

Riders are paced over a set distance either behind small scooters, known as Dernys, or, more rarely, larger motorbikes. This side of track racing is gradually dying out since its exclusion from the world championships.

TRAINING FOR THE TRACK

As with road racing, skill and technique count for as much as fitness — an experienced "trackie", no matter how unfit, will see off a fitter novice through trackcraft alone. The first essential is familiarization — getting used to riding the track in company on the fixed wheel. Pure practice on the track — in training and racing — will probably stand you in better stead than any preparation other than the work you would do building up to a season of time trials, mountain biking or road racing.

Most local trackmen do not train specifically for the track, preferring to view their one evening a week on the bankings as useful speed work that will stand them in good stead in their other racing. This in turn gives them a good base of fitness and some of the necessary skill for their track racing.

Road racing, with its emphasis on abrupt speed changes and bike handling in a group, plus the continual need to weigh up the opposition, is particularly useful for most of the bunched events you

will find at a track league. Time trials will help you acquire the ability to ride alone — vital if you are to attack to any effect in bunched events, although it should be noted that if you are to survive in the bunch time-trialling ability alone will not be of great use.

Until you decide to specialize in a particular discipline, in which case the advice you will need is outside the scope of this book, one general rule to remember is that on the track you cannot rely on pure strength to achieve high speeds — pedalling speed is the key factor. So it is key to work on what the French call "souplesse" — the ability to pedal quickly and smoothly in a low to medium gear — and this should be borne in mind as you go about your winter preparation. At a basic level, try to pedal a slightly lower gear than the man alongside you in the clubrun.

Once they have built up a foundation of suitable winter training to build on, most riders who want to spend a summer racing in a track league have no choice but to ride early season road races or time trials to work at race intensity before the track season starts in late spring. Choose short road races, preferably criteriums if you can find them, or short-distance time trials — two-ups are a good option as you will work on bike handling at the same time — and keep the gears low. Since track events are rarely longer than an hour, the emphasis must be more on speed and intensity than endurance.

The madison sling: the lead rider is "throwing" his colleague into the action to take his turn

II: RACE TRAINING

HOW DO REAL RACING CYCLISTS WITH LIVES AND JOBS GET FIT AND STAY FIT ALL YEAR ROUND, AVOIDING ILLNESS AND FATIGUE? MORE IMPORTANTLY, HOW CAN YOU LEARN FROM THEM? HERE, WE TAKE A LOOK AT FOUR REAL-LIFE CASE STUDIES ACROSS THE AGE GROUPS, ALL OF WHOM HAVE RACED SUCCESSFULLY ON OR OFF ROAD, AND SEE HOW THEY DO IT.

Theory is one thing; putting it all into practice is another. Level one, level two, interval training, sprints, racing — how do racing cyclists like you and me fit these things into their lives? How much do they train, how hard do they train and what are they trying to achieve?

If you look across the entire sphere of cyclists worldwide, you will be hard-pressed to find two who train in precisely the same way, even if they share a common age, have the same job, or race in the same branch of the sport in the same category. Two members of the same professional team may share a trainer, the same racing programme and the same goals, but their training and the way they put it into practice will not be precisely the same.

Everyone is different, aiming for different things, with different amounts of time available, and a different physique. That is why this book does not include easy-to-follow set training programmes: I feel that the best approach is to try things out with the help of a coach or an experienced fellow cyclist, and use their help and your practical experience to work out what is best for you. There are no quick, overnight remedies. Find out what works and put it into practice. If for whatever reason you don't have a coach, hopefully this book will give you some starting points.

You should aim to keep learning and experimenting throughout the time you race. It is likely that if you are starting from scratch or coming into cycling from another sport, it will take time for you to acquire the basic conditioning necessary to begin experimenting with the different kinds of training outlined in Chapters 3 and 4.

It may take several years to reach a level approaching your full potential, particularly if you are young or starting from a low fitness base. If you are under 18, you should be particularly careful about your workload. Interval training in particular is to be approached with caution and the advice of a coach.

If the opposite applies, and you have good fitness or an established programme that you have always used, it may be that some new ideas, new approaches, or some fresh feedback will give you that additional spur which enables you to get a bit more out of your bike racing.

The following case studies demonstrate how four typical amateur racing cyclists train. The studies are not intended to be blindly copied, even by those who share the same age group and ambitions. Don't read the next few pages then just go out and simply try to do the same. Look at these examples, taking particular note of how long they have been cycling compared to you. Then try and work out what you can learn from them. None of the following case studies is a full-time professional bike racer: one works full-time; one is a full-time student with a part-time job; one goes to school; one works part-time.

Jan Ullrich and Bianchi in training: long group rides like these must be seen as part of a large-scale plan

THE THIRD CATEGORY RIDER

Age: 22
Types of racing I take part in: Road racing (3rd cat) and time trialling. I have been cycling for 10 years, and racing for 6 years.
Hours available for training each week: About 14.
Other commitments: Full-time job with commute to London, shooting on Mondays and some Tuesdays, occasional night or weekend work.
Notes: I use the turbo a fair amount not only because it is frequently cold and wet outside, but also because there is more control over cadence and work load than on the road. I use a pulse monitor for training and racing. I use it a lot to ride against for time trials, but only for "interest" in road races to diagnose what is happening when I'm going well or not. In training I tend to use it to confirm what my legs are telling me and don't ride to it rigidly.

A TYPICAL WEEK IN WINTER (DECEMBER–FEBRUARY)

Day	Duration	Intensity
Monday	No training due to other commitments. I need a rest day anyway.	
Tuesday	20–30 min run/turbo If other commitments do not get in the way. Stretching before and after, duration of sessions may increase in February.	Gentle
Wednesday	If nothing on Tuesday, maybe 30 mins on turbo or swimming for an hour.	
Thursday	As Tuesday, duration according to how legs feel and how heart rate responds.	
Friday	Probably rest, as tired by work at this stage of the week.	
Saturday	40–50 miles group ride.	Level one/two
Sunday	1–2 hours easy in December, building up through January with Sunday club run so that by February I'm out every Sunday doing 2–3 hours of level 1–2.	
Comments:	The emphasis at this time of year is to give the body a rest without stopping completely and gradually build up to more intensive training in March/April. Aim is to maintain flexibility and develop good style to prevent injury. I take the weather into account — I would stay at home rather than risk a heavy fall on icy roads.	

A TYPICAL WEEK IN SPRING (MARCH–MAY)

Day	Duration	Intensity
Monday	No training due to other commitments — wouldn't do much anyway due to racing/training over weekend.	
Tuesday	2–3 hours I try to avoid other commitments and get out with a small group. Might start to include steady five-mile "through and off" sessions working up to level three.	Level two
Wednesday	1 hour Probably not too hard an evening — loosen up on the turbo for 20–30 minutes in a low gear, work steadily up to level three and back down again. Bit of stretching and a warm bath.	Level two/three
Thursday	2–3 hours Similar to Tuesday but shorter because everyone is starting to feel tired. Might go harder for the first half, then steady for the rest.	Level two
Friday	Nothing — recovery before the weekend.	
Saturday	Varies If no race on Sunday, the usual café run at level one, but distance increasing to 50–60 miles, with maybe the odd 10 minutes at level three. If racing on Sunday, then rest.	Varies
Sunday	1–3 hours Maybe a hilly time trial or "25" — I usually start road racing during May, but only if I feel ready for it. Time trials are testing grounds to judge form — I usually ride them on the road bike. If not racing, then club ride or 60–70 miles with a tea stop.	Race/club ride
Comments	This is where serious work begins, joining the winter and the season. It can be hard getting out after work due to difficulty in eating enough at lunchtime. Duration/work levels during rides increase — start to use higher gears to increase strength.	

A TYPICAL WEEK IN SUMMER (JUNE–AUGUST)

Day	Duration	Intensity
Monday	No training due to other commitments — wouldn't do much anyway due to racing/training over weekend.	
Tuesday	3 hours Chaingang for about two hours. Steady for first and last 30 mins with continuous level three in between, creeping into level four. A hard session — slaughters me, but is of great benefit.	Level two/three
Wednesday	1 hour Probably a gentle session on the turbo or more likely on the road. Quite steady level two/three, but not so the legs hurt too much after chaingang on Tuesday. As much effort as is comfortable.	Level two/three
Thursday	30 mins Club evening "10" — for continuous speed training, not specifically for time trialling, but for situations where might be off front of a road race. A useful short, sharp session, and fun, which is what it is all about.	Level three
Friday	Varies Probably a very light session on the turbo to loosen up and ride out the evening "10" from Thursday.	Level one
Saturday	Varies If no racing, café run as usual. If racing on Sunday, nothing on the bike. Saturday is all about food and I usually go well on a steak. Plenty of fluids, but no beer.	Varies
Sunday	Race	Race
Comments	As I'm concentrating on racing, training is directed at ticking over between racing and working on weaknesses. I sometimes use races, especially criteriums as training — spend more time on the front, chase more often, or practice technique. ·	

A TYPICAL WEEK IN AUTUMN (SEPTEMBER–NOVEMBER)

Day	Duration	Intensity
Monday	No training due to other commitments — wouldn't do much anyway due to racing/training over weekend.	
Tuesday	Varies Probably continue with chaingang until they stop in September. In October and November I will probably start running at lunchtime or in the evening, mainly off the roads. Nothing too strenuous at first as it is so different to cycling.	Varies
Wednesday	Varies If I'm still racing, a short spinning session on the road or the turbo. If I've packed in racing — nothing.	Level one/two
Thursday	Varies Either a light turbo session if still racing, or a run at level two/three.	Varies
Friday	Quite likely don't do anything, especially if I've stopped racing. I might go for a short run (20 mins).	
Saturday	Nothing today if I'm racing tomorrow, otherwise the café run, even if I'm training for running, just to keep the legs turning.	
Sunday	60–90 mins Possibly a race during September, but in October/November a longer run of 60-90 minutes at a steady pace or a cross-country race of about six miles.	Run
Comments	I don't usually race after September and then only if I'm going well. Training winds down anyway as if there is no form now it's too late. By the end of November I start to ride more again as too much running weakens cycling muscles. Weekly café ride is to try to counter this. The real goal is to do something different and have a mental break.	

THE VETERAN

Age: 48
Types of racing I take part in: Road racing (veterans local, plus national series). I have been cycling for 10 years, and racing for 5 years. Before that I played football. I had three knee operations and decided that cycling was the best thing for my knees. I started with a couple of miles on my wife's shopping bike and gradually got into it.
Hours available for training each week: About 20.
Other commitments: Work etc. I work from home, which is flexible and allows me to fit it around training.
Notes: I tend not to follow levels (i.e. heart rate) too rigidly as I often ride on how I feel. Experience with the heart rate monitor has taught me that I can judge my pulse quite accurately by how I feel. I do not stick to a schedule either. I tend to rest more than the questionnaire indicates. Starting out as a vet has advantages — you have the enthusiasm of a junior, but you're racing with people who've raced for a long time and are more circumspect. It's all fresh and new and motivating. The disadvantage is that you don't have the experience of a long-time cyclist, so you have to learn quite quickly. The great benefit as you get older is that cycling is not load-bearing so the problems you have when you're older with joints etc. don't come into play as with other sports. Stamina and a good engine means that you can keep going and get great satisfaction from beating people half your age. The only disadvantage is that it takes a while to warm up, and it takes a long time to find form.

A TYPICAL WEEK IN WINTER (DECEMBER–JANUARY)

Day	Duration	Intensity
Monday	Rest	
Tuesday	1 hour Turbo session. I try to get to level three for a decent length of time, but the higher the intensity the shorter the ride ends up. The problem with the turbo is that you can get addicted, so I try after Christmas to go out in the evening.	Level two/three
Wednesday	4–5 hours I constantly try to get into level two — the majority of the ride is at that intensity, but I actually find it harder by myself than with a group at weekends.	Level two
Thursday	3 hours The same as Wednesday. These rides are for building a base — towards the season I sharpen them up a bit, but I find the turbo session brings me on most.	Level two
Friday	90 mins A recovery ride. If the weather's not up to it I have another rest because I know the weekend is coming up. It's for morale as much as anything else, or if I've missed a day in the week.	Level one
Saturday	3.5 hours A group ride to a café — I lead them so I have an advantage in that I can dictate the route.	Level one/two
Sunday	4–5 hours Typically, out of four or five hours, three-and-a-half or four will be in level two. This is a group ride with a café stop, but towards the beginning of the season I don't stop, because the sustained period of level two is of real benefit.	Level 2
Comments	In this period I'm trying to build a good base. Because of my age I try to keep from slipping downhill. I have to improve just to stand still. I vary the miles with different terrains — different hills. As the winter goes on it just seems to get faster and easier and the gears get higher.	

A TYPICAL WEEK IN SPRING (FEBRUARY–MARCH)

Day	Duration	Intensity
Monday	Rest	
Tuesday	1 hour (turbo) If I'm on the turbo I try never to do the same thing — sometimes it's basic intervals, sometimes 10 minutes level one, 10 minutes level three. I have to build very slowly to level three.	Level two/three
Wednesday	4–5 hours I keep this ride pretty much the same all year round. It's a data point — I can see if I'm getting fitter, how I feel, according to whether I want to go up the hills or not…	Level two

Thursday	1 hour (turbo) This is a really hard one, to bring myself on. I simulate a circuit race, with short intense efforts and traditional intervals. One programme I use is from a Danish pro, John Carlsen, where you go at 80 per cent of maximum heart rate. You have two minute rests and do five minutes twice, then four minutes twice, three minutes twice, then two minutes twice, then you're sick! It gets more intense as the season gets nearer — I may add 30 second sprints.	Level three/four
Friday	2 hours This is not essential — I miss it if I'm feeling at all tired.	Level two
Saturday	3.5 hours This is the café run — just a relaxed ride. If I'm racing the next day, just level one.	Level one/two
Sunday	4–5 hours I start racing in late March, otherwise this is as before.	Level two or race
Comments	This period is where I build on what has gone before and bridge to racing. In the past I've done a couple of two-up time trials just before racing — they're great for getting your heart up and getting some speed in.	

A TYPICAL WEEK IN SUMMER (JUNE–AUGUST)

Day	Duration	Intensity
Monday	Rest	
Tuesday	90 minutes (chaingang) This is good for speed and the road-racing rhythm of "through and off". After about 10 minutes I get into it — the first 10 I struggle, then it still hurts but feels rhythmic. Mostly level three, slipping into level four.	Level three/four
Wednesday	3–4 hours It depends how I am in general and what races are coming up. If I know there are long, hilly races coming up I go and find long climbs for a few weeks before. Normally it's level two, with level three over the climbs.	Varies
Thursday	2–3 hours Usually I ride out to an evening circuit race, ride and then ride home.	All levels
Friday	90 mins–2 hours This depends on what else I'm doing, how tired I am, what's coming up at the weekend.	Level one/two
Saturday	2 hours Sometimes I race, but usually my son races, so I just fit in a race of some kind. I can miss this one out, especially if it's a big race next day.	Level one
Sunday	Race	Race
Comments	I do a lot less training at this time, I tend to look for the right sort of racing midweek to work on weaknesses. I'm no good at sprinting so I ride a circuit race to work on it. I ride at Milton Keynes Bowl — you have to sprint every lap up a little hill. It's better than sprint training on the road — there's more of an edge.	

A TYPICAL WEEK IN AUTUMN (SEPTEMBER–NOVEMBER)

Day	Duration	Intensity
Monday	Rest	
Tuesday	Rest	
Wednesday	3 hours I keep at a level where I reckon I'm burning fat, which is just below level two where I can feel I'm making an effort and concentrating. The other thing I do is try to sit down on all the hills — it's not something I do enough in races.	Level one/two
Thursday	Race	
Friday	Race	
Saturday	3 hours This is the café run — I try to keep at level one, but it doesn't always end up like that.	Level one
Sunday	4 hours	Level one/two
Comments	This is when I just tick over and try to have a good time — enjoying it rather than thrashing it. I try not to put on weight, but it doesn't always work out like that.	

THE SCHOOLBOY

Age: 15
Types of racing I take part in: Criteriums, time trials, track. I have been cycling for eight years, and racing for four-and-a-half years. Approximate number of hours I have available for training each week 10—15
Other commitments: Schoolwork at various times, e.g. exams.
Notes: I keep my training short because the races are short — when the national road-race championship comes around in the summer I do longer rides, because that is 30 miles. The track and circuit races are never longer than 10 miles, and I never do more than a 10-mile time trial — maybe next year when I'm 16. I've got GCSEs and the short rides can be fitted in around the schoolwork. I never do recreational rides except in winter — in summer if you're going to be on the bike, you might as well be training. I never get stale because of all the different kinds of races. The track is very useful — I used not to be very good at sprinting, and juvenile races are quite fast, but that's not a problem now. When I started I was doing a three-mile race once a week, and was riding once or twice a week to enjoy myself. I didn't take racing seriously — if I got better placings, or only got lapped twice or whatever, I was happy. Losing as a juvenile doesn't matter — the big, strong guys who win everything at 14 or 15 find the transfer to junior level very difficult.

A TYPICAL WEEK IN WINTER (DECEMBER—FEBRUARY)

Day	Duration	Intensity
Monday	Nothing	
Tuesday	Nothing	
Wednesday	0.5 hour At the end of the winter I do this to build up a bit of fitness — I'll do short sprints or have a five-minute warm-up and then go hard for 25 minutes.	Level three
Thursday	Nothing	
Friday	Nothing	
Saturday	Nothing	
Sunday	60 miles This is usually a club run with a café stop. If I'm with the older riders, it's mainly level two.	Level one/two
Comments	It's too dark at this time of year after school to do much, so I rely on the sport I do at school for general fitness.	

A TYPICAL WEEK IN SPRING (MARCH—MAY)

Day	Duration	Intensity
Monday	Rest	
Tuesday	90 minutes I have a circuit of between 20 and 25 miles which I do at just below time-trial pace.	Level three
Wednesday	Rest Sometimes in May I go out if I feel good — it depends if I've got any big races coming up, such as the schoolboy national title.	
Thursday	30—45 minutes I sprint as hard as I can every three minutes, then I ride fairly easy to recover, then go again.	Level three or four — sprints
Friday	Rest	
Saturday	45 minutes I race alternate weekends, so if I'm not racing I go hard for half an hour, almost at time-trial pace after a warm-up.	Race
Sunday	Varies In early spring I'll go on a clubrun, or go out with a friend. It's not as intense, so it builds up the stamina a bit. But from late April I'll do an hour at time-trial pace.	Varies
Comments	I start in earnest in late March or early April, which is when I do most of my build-up. I can't ride every day in summer when I'm relying on races to get me fit. By spring I can go out most evenings after school.	

A TYPICAL WEEK IN SUMMER (JUNE–AUGUST)

Day	Duration	Intensity
Monday	2 hours This is track training at my local track — we ride round in a group, the whistle blows in the back straight, and we sprint for half a lap, then there's a big sprint at the end. This gets me pretty tired.	Sprints — at track
Tuesday	Rest	
Wednesday	30 mins This varies with rest if it was a hard weekend. I take my pulse in the morning and go from there depending how I feel.	Level three
Thursday	30 mins Club evening "10".	High level three
Friday	2 hours I began with the juvenile races, which are all short, plus the 10-mile senior event at the end of the evening if I wasn't racing at the weekend. Now I've moved up to the B-cat races, which is three 10-lap races in the evening.	Track racing
Saturday	1 hour	Level three or race
Sunday	1 hour	Level three or race
Comments	I race and train on alternate weekends, either Saturday or Sunday, so whenever I'm not racing I train if there's something big coming up, or I rest. Usually there's something like a time trial or a big track race coming up.	

A TYPICAL WEEK IN AUTUMN (SEPTEMBER–NOVEMBER)

Day	Duration	Intensity
Monday	Rest	
Tuesday	1 hour	Level three
Wednesday	Rest	
Thursday	30 mins	Upper level three
Friday	Rest	
Saturday	Race I usually stop racing in mid-September, and after that I probably won't do very much at all.	Race
Sunday	40 miles This is just a relaxed group ride with the club.	Level two
Comments	In September and October I do a bit on the turbo, and in November and December I just do one weekend ride. Generally from autumn to spring I'm doing PE at school and a bit of cross-country running which keeps me fit.	

The bunch in a road race fans out up a climb: the pressure isn't on, but the effort can be read on the faces

THE WOMAN MOUNTAIN BIKER

Age: 20

Types of racing I take part in: Mountain-biking cross-country; road racing; time trials; cyclo-cross. I have been cycling for two-and-a-half years, and racing for two-and-a-half years.

Hours available for training each week: 12–15 hours. I am prepared to make available as much time as necessary.

Other commitments: I am a full-time degree student in politics at London University, where I need to be for two days a week. Also a part-time waitressing job on Friday and Saturday nights — this is quite tiring, so if I have an important race I take time off.

Notes: In the past year my training has become a lot more structured, with rides being more defined (a recovery ride is now very easy, and a level two ride feels like hard work). Much of this is due to the help and advice I receive from my coach. His advice has a "controlling" effect on my tendency to overtrain, which at my age I understand is important to avoid. Each year my training has included more high intensity work, and in winter the volume has increased too with more split training and running. The emphasis on my year-to-year training is one of steady progression by establishing a solid quality endurance base — this steady progression is evident in my results. My training year is pretty constant — I only ease up in late September when I take a few easy weeks. I am prepared to ease up between October and December if I get tired, since at this time of year I don't want to feel worn down. I feel that my body is better able to cope with training like this now and I feel increasingly more focused not only in training, but in everyday self-discipline e.g. diet, time organization.

A TYPICAL WEEK IN WINTER (DECEMBER–JANUARY)

Day	Duration	Intensity
Monday	90 mins–2 hours If I am tired, a total rest day. Very easy spinning — either commuting to university and back or around the lanes.	Level one
Tuesday a.m.	30 mins Steady cross-country run followed by stretching.	Running
Tuesday p.m.	2 hours/30–35 miles Around one of a number of set routes to gauge progress.	Level two
Wednesday	Varies Either weights and gym work — light weights for the upper body, plus 20 minutes level three on an exercise bike — or 90 minutes level two on the road with 4–6 one-minute sprints.	Varies
Thursday	90 mins–2 hours As Monday — a steady recovery ride.	Level one
Friday a.m.	40 minutes As Tuesday.	Running
Friday p.m.	1 hour	Level one
Saturday	2 hours/35 miles Around a set route with lots of medium-length hills, which I go hard up. If I'm racing on Sunday I cut the distance and time.	Level two — hard
Sunday	Varies Either a cyclo-cross race or a long steady (level one/two) mountain-bike or road ride with friends.	Varies
Comments	This period is usually interrupted by a holiday at Christmas when I take my bike but usually do much longer rides and have a less structured plan. One Christmas I was in Los Angeles for a month and did a lot of riding with other people at high intensity. Another time I went to Spain. I believe that training "midwinter" somewhere warm where you can wear shorts and a short-sleeve jersey helps to put "zip" back into your legs as the seemingly never-ending cold and wet rides in England become a bit of a trudge.	

A TYPICAL WEEK IN SPRING (FEBRUARY–APRIL)

Day	Duration	Intensity
Monday	1 hour Recovery ride — maybe to university and back.	Level one
Tuesday	2 hours/30–35 miles Maintaining a constant hard pace around one of several set routes, all quite hilly.	Level two
Wednesday	90 mins (40 mins turbo) A ride down to a bike park in central London where I put my bike on the turbo trainer and do three times seven minutes at level three with three-minute recovery in between. There may be variations on this.	Varied

Thursday	2 hours/30–35 miles As Tuesday.	Level two
Friday a.m.	40 mins Long, steady cross-country run.	Running
Friday p.m.	1 hour–90 mins Steady recovery ride.	Level one
Saturday	Varies Either a race – late in spring this will probably be a criterium or a time trial, but early on it's more likely to be two hours level two, with some sprints.	Varies
Sunday	1 hour–90 mins Late in spring this will be a race like that on Saturday, but early in spring it is more likely to be a mountain-bike ride concentrating on technique.	Mountain bike or race
Comments	This is a difficult time to do a "typical week" in since it is really a transition stage between winter and summer training with lots of level two and some turbo training, which may vary between short and long intervals and longer level three workouts. I may also do some hill sprint training at this stage – running is cut back and weight training cut out.	

A TYPICAL WEEK IN SUMMER (JUNE–AUGUST)

Day	Duration	Intensity
Monday	1 hour–90 mins Recovery ride with small gears. My legs are usually tired so this is just to enjoy the countryside.	Level one
Tuesday	45–90 minutes Either a 10-mile time trial with warm-up or a level one and two ride. If it has been a really tough race on Sunday, it may even be a recovery ride.	Varies
Wednesday	90 mins/27 miles A low level two ride spinning fast gears and keeping steady. If there was no time trial on Tuesday, it may be a bit longer.	Low level two
Thursday	75 mins/26 miles Evening circuit race with third category men, juniors and veterans. How much work I do depends on my legs – if I feel tired I sit in the bunch, otherwise I try to work at the front more.	Race + warm-up
Friday	Rest	
Saturday	Varies Sometimes a race, sometimes a two-hour level two ride, or a couple of laps of the course for a Sunday mountain-bike race. It's flexible, depending on what I've done during the week.	Varies
Sunday	Race	Race
Comments	Increasingly I use races to maintain form in summer, using evening criteriums and time trials as training races. I find this more fun – even though I may race three or four times a week I seem to stay fresh if I do little training on the other days. If I have a big race coming up I may race four times the week before – a very hard week – and then ease up in the week leading up to the race, cutting out all long rides and maybe doing one or two 90-minute "punchy" rides.	

A TYPICAL WEEK IN AUTUMN (SEPTEMBER–NOVEMBER)

Day	Duration	Intensity
Monday	90 mins–2 hours As in "winter" – either to and from university or around the lanes.	Level one
Tuesday a.m.	30–40 mins Steady cross-country run followed by stretching.	Running
Tuesday p.m.	90 minutes/28–30 miles This is a level two ride, with four to six short jumps going into level three. I usually do one of a few "set" routes to gauge progress, hope to maintain a speed around 18–19mph, and usually take in a few hills.	Level two
Wednesday a.m.	30 mins Steady cross-country run followed by stretching.	Running
Wednesday p.m.	An easy ride to the gym and back, where I do 20 minutes level three on the turbo bike, and about one hour weight-training using light weights for my upper body. I sometimes also row or climb for 20 minutes: every fourth week the level three ride is taken out and I just ride over and do weights. If I am a little tired I sometimes do sprint intervals (six times 1–2 minutes) on the turbo instead.	

Thursday	90 mins–2 hours Commuting to college and back, mainly easy.	Level one
Friday a.m.	30–40 mins Steady cross-country run followed by stretching.	Running
Friday p.m.	1 hour Recovery ride around the lanes — very easy spinning, sometimes left out.	Level one
Saturday	1 hour 50 minutes/33 miles Hard level two around a set hilly route — this ride is substituted with one similar to Tuesday if I am racing on Sunday.	Level two
Sunday	Varies Either a cyclo-cross race, towards the end of autumn, or a three- to four-hour steady road-bike or mountain-bike ride with friends, and at varying intensities.	Varies
Comments	At this time of year every fourth week is made easier by removing level three on Wednesday, or making Friday a rest day, or not running on Wednesday — any or all three may be taken out, depending on how I feel. I try to race only three weeks out of four to get in some long rides, and race more in November/December than in September/October when I don't race.	

CONCLUSIONS

A brief look at all four of the examples shows various points that it is worth considering when you are planning your training and racing.

AM I PREPARED TO BE FLEXIBLE?

Unless you are a full-time professional (in which case you won't be reading this!) you have to allow for the possibility that you will sometimes be better off resting than training. This is something that must be built in when you plan your training. Slavishly following a schedule rarely works. If your work routine is erratic, base your training around a certain number of core sessions during the week on the specific areas you need to improve — sprinting, threshold, mountain-bike skills perhaps — and use any remaining time for endurance work at level one and level two.

IS MY TRAINING RACE-SPECIFIC?

A look at the juvenile and veteran, father and son, shows this point. The father is riding 90-mile veterans' road races, so he spends a winter doing "long, steady, distance" miles to build stamina. His 15-year-old son rarely races over one hour, so he bases his training around intense efforts no longer than that. It sounds obvious, but if you are racing already when you read this, ask yourself: is my training appropriate for the kind of racing I am doing?

AM I WORKING ON MY WEAKNESSES?

Be honest with yourself in identifying weak areas and working on them. Our veteran admits that sprinting, and dealing with changes of speed in road races are weak points, so he rides a midweek circuit race, where the short, intense efforts will help him improve.

WHY AM I DOING THIS SESSION?

Whenever you go to train, have an idea of what you are going to achieve during that session, and, if possible, how it fits into the broader picture of where you are going over the season. For example, at a simple level: "This is a ride where I am going to try to do two hours at level two including 15 minutes at level three. Last week I did the same ride, without the level three, which I need to introduce as the racing season approaches."

This does not mean that every time you go out on your bike you must be in "training mode" or feel you have to train. That way lies overtraining, disillusionment and an early exit from cycling. Do not be afraid to say to yourself, "I'm just going out to ride."

AM I TRAINING HARD ENOUGH?

You'll notice that all the case studies include intense training sessions — mainly at level three or "time-trial pace". If you have a good base of endurance riding, don't feel that racing alone will give you the intense workouts you need to improve.

AM I TRAINING TOO HARD?

The balance between intense training and rest is the key to success. Don't be afraid to abandon an intense session if you feel you are not up to it. Overtraining is a greater danger than undertraining.

AM I RESTING ENOUGH?

All the case studies include days off in their routines. If you find that you cannot train at the intensity you intend to, or you are performing poorly in races, or tend to get ill frequently, analyse whether you rest sufficiently to recover from training and racing. Perhaps you need more sleep, more time doing nothing, or less training.

CAN I DO ANYTHING ELSE?

Running is an old favourite — great for heart and lungs, not so good for cycling-specific muscles. It's crucial anyway if you are racing cyclo-cross or mountain bike. Stretch afterwards. Weight-training can be helpful with the advice of a coach. Rowing is excellent for the upper body, but beware of building muscle bulk that will be a handicap on two wheels. All year round, but particularly in the off-season, any low-impact endurance exercise is beneficial, for your state of mind as well as your fitness — for example hill-walking, circuit training or cross-country skiing.

12: THE START LINE

READY TO RACE? NOT QUITE. IF YOU GET YOUR PRE-RACE ROUTINE DOWN TO A "T", YOUR CHANCES OF SUCCESS WILL IMPROVE, AND IF YOU KNOW WHAT'S GOING IN YOUR KIT-BAG, YOU'LL TAKE MUCH OF THE STRESS OUT OF GETTING TO YOUR RACE. AND HOW MUCH SLEEP DO YOU NEED, PLUS, THE BIGGEST QUESTION OF ALL: WHAT ABOUT SEX BEFORE RACING?

THINK AHEAD

You have trained hard; you have a bike that fits and functions. You have set your goals. Now it's time to get in the saddle and try to beat the world. Would that it were quite as simple as that. Unfortunately, it is possible to lose a race between finishing your last serious training session and watching the start flag drop.

If you devote a little time to getting organized and planning what you're going to do before you head for that pasta party on a northern moor or that village hall in Much Nowhere, you will find you have more energy to devote to what really matters — the race itself.

The better organized you are, the less chance there is that unforeseen mishaps can occur to distract you from the business in hand. On the ideal race day, you should be able to eat, prepare your race drinks, then walk out of the house, picking up kit bag and bike on the way, get into the car and go. The night and the morning before a race should become a routine into which you slip automatically. This reduction of the stress involved in racing will make competing more pleasurable, as well as, ideally, more successful.

ENTERING RACES IN ADVANCE

The first element of a stress-free build-up to a race is to enter in advance whenever you can if there is likely to be any restriction on numbers. Then you will know what race you are doing and when, and you will have some idea of what to expect. In mountain biking and road racing you will save money if you pre-enter as well.

Where road racing is concerned, relying solely on races that you can enter "on the line" is a rather seat-of-

the pants approach: it means that there can be some uncertainty as to whether you will ride, which in turn does not help you get organized beforehand. If you are planning your season in advance, you should know what you are doing and when.

Entry formalities, fees and deadlines vary across British racing. Here, however, is a quick user's guide:

TIME TRIALS

Club time trials are run on an enter-on-the-day basis, while "open" events listed in the *RTTC Handbook* — that is to say the bulk of weekend races — must be entered in advance.

- Entry fee — £8–10.
- Entry forms — Cycling Time Trials issue, available from club secretaries.
- Deadline for entries — two weeks.
- Must previous performances be included on the form? Yes — fastest times may be used to select the field if the race is oversubscribed.
- Will they put you down as a reserve? No.

MOUNTAIN-BIKE RACES

These vary between organizers, but most cross-country events can be entered on the day, although pre-entry is preferable, while most downhill events need to be pre-entered.

- Entry fee — for cross-country, between £15–£25. For downhill, between £20–£45.
- Entry forms — usually direct from organizers or via websites.
- Deadline for entries — varies.
- Must previous performances be included on form? No, because outside the highest levels, the sport is age-based.
- Restrictions on numbers? Usually only at downhill events.

CYCLO-CROSS

Apart from the National Championships, all cyclo-cross races can and should be entered on the day.

ROAD RACES

With one or two exceptions, all road races listed in the BC calendar can be pre-entered. Entering in advance is strongly recommended for weekend races, which are usually held on the open road and are therefore subject to restrictions on numbers. At many midweek races, usually held on circuits away from the open road so with no limitation on the size of the field, you can turn up and enter on the day.

Many weekend road races can be entered on the day, but these are often over-subscribed, and you may well be turned away disappointed. If you have to enter a weekend road race on the day, it's best to call the organizer to find out whether the race is "full" or not.

- Entry fee — between £8 and £20.
- Entry forms — BCF issue, available from club secretaries.
- Deadline for entries in advance — three weeks.
- Must previous best performances be included on form? Yes, and they may be used to select the field if the race is oversubscribed.
- Will they put you down as a reserve? Up to 10 reserves are selected for road races with a limited field. It's always worth turning up if you are a reserve — usually enough riders fail to turn up for you to get a ride.

TRACK RACES

Only major track meetings have to be entered in advance. The rest of the time you can just turn up and enter on the day.

The author in the Etape du Tour: bike in order, body as ready as it ever will be

- Inspect the brake blocks for wear, especially if you have been racing in the wet, and make sure all brake and gear cables run smoothly and are not showing signs of fraying.
- Is there any play in the brakes — are they still properly adjusted to the rims?
- Run through the gears — do they index perfectly? Is the chain looking worn?
- Check whether the wheels are true as they run between the brake blocks, and flex the spokes gently — are any loose, even if the wheel is true?
- Is there any movement where the brake levers join the bars?
- Are the chainring bolts tight? Are any chainring teeth bent?
- Is there any movement in the bottle cage(s)?
- Double-check everything if you've had a crash.

By looking over your machine immediately after you race it, you have six full days to clear up any problems, either on your own or at your local bike shop.

Leaving your inspection of the bike until the day before you need it — even if it has raced perfectly — can be a recipe for severe stress, which is just what you don't want before racing, and possibly a botched repair that could turn your race into a disaster. The same applies to changes of position — don't, at any price, do them the day before a race.

WHAT DO I TAKE?

One top professional team manager famously commented that he could tell the quality of a racer by the size of his suitcase. If he was a "large suitcase man", by implication a disorganized chap who took all sorts of clutter with him, he was not going to make the grade. A "small suitcase man" was what was wanted.

Suitcase size matters most when you are a professional racer flying around Europe, but the manager was right. You will get a lot further if you work out what you are going to need and make sure you have it ready to hand, rather than packing the kitchen sink into a bag on the off-chance that you may need it to wash a dirty sock in.

Racing bags have infinite ramifications according to the manufacturer's whim, but the ideal bag will

You may have to pre-register with your local track league.

THE BIKE

The most common pre-race problems are "mechanicals": a worn brake block, for example, or a creaking cable that you decide to look at "just in case" and which reveals a more serious problem. The last thing you want on a race morning is to have to work against the clock to make a couple of minor adjustments to the bike.

As mentioned previously, the time to check your bike is after a race, and a quick once-over should become part of your post-race routine, along with washing your kit and feeding bottles: this

may not be pleasant when you're tired, but you will feel the better for it. Once the bike is clean, the shorts are in the washing machine and the bottles are drying on the draining board, it's easier to rest — the race is totally behind you.

This should be your checklist when you wash the bike down after a race:

- Check the tyres for wear, cuts, or flints or thorns that have lodged in the casing, and make sure they haven't deflated more than you would expect. You could have picked up a slow puncture during the race which, if you don't find it now, will become evident only when you look the bike over before the next race.

A pro team prepares to take the road: as an amateur you may not have all the kit, but you can still get organized

have at least four compartments: one for flat items such as licence and startsheet, one for items that can spill, one for smallish items you don't want to lose, and a large, principal compartment for clothing.

Pack your bag the night before the race if you are leaving in the morning: whatever you do, don't leave it until just before you depart. Inevitably one sock — or a vital item such as your helmet — will have hidden itself in an obscure part of the house, whereupon you will spend 20 minutes looking for it and will leave in a flustered, unhappy state. If you know the bag is ready, you can relax in the morning, pick it up and go.

It is also worth making sure you know where you are racing, and have figured out how long it will take to get there, building in some time for delays. This sounds obvious, but at every race I ever rode, at least one rider turned up late or got lost en route to the start.

The checklist for all types of races should include:

- Your race clothing: shoes, socks, shorts, jersey, undervest, track mitts, arm- or leg-warmers depending on the time of year, and helmet. Listen to the weather forecast, and put in things like cold-weather gloves and warm under-jersey if it sounds even slightly dubious.
- Glasses with change of lenses for rain or sun.
- Racing licence.
- Start sheet or directions for getting to the race.
- Warm-up rub or embrocation. Cater for rain and cold weather, when you will need a lanolin rub, which keeps your legs and arms warm. Similarly, if it's bright sunshine and you burn easily, take some sport-type sun block.
- Clean-up kit, including shower gel and shampoo if there are likely to be shower facilities; towel; facecloth; antiseptic soap solution for cleaning embrocation off your hands before the race and rubbing yourself down afterwards if there are no showers.
- Race food — prepare any bottles you will need before you leave, and carry them outside the race bag, as they will inevitably leak if put next to your kit. Carry more food than you need, so that you can eat some afterwards.
- Safety pins for fixing number.
- Toilet paper.
- Flipflops for the showers.

An optional extra if you have space would be a small first-aid kit consisting of antiseptic spray, gauze and plasters, so that you can treat abrasions from any minor crash (on the principle that if you have it, hopefully you won't need it).

Road racers and time triallists should take wet-weather kit consisting of rain gloves, overshoes and oversocks, rain cape and a plastic shopping bag to put wet clothing in after the race.

Road racers riding a stage race will want to add to the list: a duplicate set of race clothing for each stage; a spare crash hat; spare shoes; extra washing gear and race food as appropriate.

Time triallists should bear in mind the possible lack of anywhere to change and take suitable precautions, such as pulling on race shorts under a tracksuit to wear in the car if the journey to the start is a short one.

Track racers probably won't need the wet-weather kit, but should include an ample supply of undervests and shorts, if riding several races in one session; also tracksuit bottoms and a warm top to wear between races.

Mountain-bike and cyclo-cross racers will want to bear in mind possible lack of changing facilities. Maybe you don't need the kitchen sink, but you could take a can of water to wash in. Extra warm clothing for standing around afterwards, wet weather gear, and a hat are a good idea, as are plastic bags for filthy and wet clothing — even if it's a dry day, you may have a river crossing or a muddy place to race through. For some mountain-bike series, you may have to keep the same number or number plate for the bike.

TOOL KIT

Like the basic first-aid kit, you should not need it, but Murphy's Law might dictate that something goes wrong before you get to the start line if you don't put it into the car with the bike. If you are a road racer riding a small stage race, take extra spares to allow for eventualities such as punctures and bear in mind the need to clean off the bike if it rains.

If you are racing off-road, a bare minimum of bucket, brush and a jerry-can of water will enable you to get the

It's all about attention to detail: here Lance Armstrong checks his saddle angle before a time trial

worst of the dirt off the bike before you put it in the car. Otherwise, it will dry as you go home and drop off the bike into the car. For a mountain bike race where you may be riding the course one day, and racing the next, take spares in case anything gets damaged or out of kilter during course inspection.

PRE-RACE ROUTINE

The night before a race, get the bag packed and give the bike one final check — more for peace of mind than in the expectation of actually finding anything wrong. Work on the principle that the less you have to do the next day the better, so get anything else you may need ready.

What to eat before a race, and what to take with you to eat and drink are dealt with in Chapter 5. However, it is worth noting here that you probably don't want to make up drinks of the powdered carbohydrate (Maxim, Hi5, PSP) type the night before a race: some riders have complained that these can go off even if refrigerated, so it's better to make them up in the morning. But make sure your bottles and tub of powdered drink are ready and waiting.

Don't be obsessive about what time

you get to bed — some trainers believe that the amount of sleep you get two nights before a race is actually more important. The rest you have or have not had during the week will make more of an impact than an hour more or less the night before. Simply make sure you are properly rested, without going to bed so early that you lie there all night worrying. And the old wives' tales about no sex before racing are pure mythology, as long as you still get the hours of sleep you need.

Mountain-bike racers should pre-ride the course at least once if it is permitted, preferably more than that, and certainly several times if it is a downhill rather than a cross-country event. To allow time for this, avoiding the other races that may be held on the same day, and during which you are not allowed to ride the course, most mountain-bike riders go to the course the previous day, and stay nearby overnight.

On the day, allow more time than you need to get to the start — think about things like local traffic conditions, roadworks, etc. You can cut it fine if you're organized, but the nervous moments experienced on the way make this a dubious approach. Save your

nervous energy for the race rather than wasting it driving to the start like Michael Schumacher.

Bear in mind that even after you have arrived at the village or town you will have to find the race headquarters — it may not be perfectly signposted.

For road races, you have to "sign on" — surrender your licence and sign the disclaimer sheet — 20 minutes before the start, and this is usually strictly adhered to. This means you should aim to arrive a minimum of 30 minutes before the cut-off time, i.e. just under one hour before the start. Evening circuit races can be a little more flexible, but you still don't want to be rushing.

Similarly, at any mountain-bike race, it may take a good while to negotiate the registration queue. There are set times for signing on for the various categories, usually about two hours before race start. Check with your entry details.

More relaxed events such as cyclo-cross, track and time trials are a little more flexible, but allow yourself more time than you need so that the minutiae such as parking, putting the bike together and warming up are not stressful owing to pressure of time. The less energy you waste on trivia before the race, the more you have left to concentrate on the business of racing.

You may find it helps to take an extra bottle of your race drink to glug down in the car on the way to your race, particularly in hot weather.

WARMING UP

As already mentioned in Chapter 10, "warming up" — riding for a short while before the race so that the effort does not come as a complete shock to your body — is of particular importance if you are riding a time trial, where you will lose valuable time if your body is not prepared to ride almost flat out from the word "go".

However, in any race, warming up should be a part of your pre-event routine that you never miss out. The first few minutes after the start can be of vital importance in mountain-bike and cyclo-cross races, track events and criteriums,

Warming-up is crucial before a cyclo-cross: here the Dutch team prepare on home trainers

Even world champions have to register before a race: the 2002 title holder "SuperMario" Cipollini puts pen to paper

while almost every road race contains one courageous soul who wakes up the field with an early attack. Many of the riders who lose contact early in a road race do so because they have not warmed up and cannot cope when the first acceleration is made. Arriving in plenty of time allows you to get a relaxed, long warm-up.

For many riders, rubbing embrocation into the legs is a vital part of the warm-up process, but it is important not just to put on any old stuff you pick up at the chemist's: on cold days, some products that cause the blood vessels to dilate or that irritate the skin to make you "feel" warm will actually cause you to lose body heat. For rain or cold, therefore, you should look for a rub containing

lanolin, which will actually protect the legs to some extent. Even baby oil can be used. If it's really cold, use it on the arms as well.

A protective rub is intended to inhibit heat loss from the legs, so you may not want to put on anything at all in warm weather if you find you suffer from the heat. However, many riders find it is a formality that they cannot do without.

It should be noted that rubbing your legs with some fine-smelling substance may bring blood into the muscles and relax the legs, but it won't do anything for your heart and lungs, which have to be warmed up on the road.

You should warm up for at least 20 minutes: after a few minutes' easy riding,

you should include some time at which you are riding at race pace — if you have a pulse monitor, the pulse rate at which you would ride a time trial. How much work is put in at this increased pace is down to the individual and the event — more for a short-distance time trial, a cyclo-cross, a mountain bike race or criterium, less for a long road race, where you will not want to burn up energy unnecessarily. Experiment — but don't try not warming up. Eventually you will know what is right for you. If you are racing off-road, include some short climbs.

The only circumstance in which you can warm up for a slightly shorter period is before a road race with a few kilometres "neutralized" at the start, where you are confident you can use the first few accelerations to adapt to full race pace, and where the start is flat. In this situation, if that suits you, take a simple "leg-stretcher" with a few sprints to loosen up the legs.

But breaks have been known to go in the neutralized zone, and you will only have yourself to blame if the first break is the winning one and you are not in it because you are not warmed up.

If you are riding a cyclo-cross, a short-course mountain-bike race, or a criterium, use the warm-up period to familiarize yourself with the course. Ride round at least once, preferably two or three times, looking out for anything that might take you by surprise in the heat of the race.

- If the weather is cold or wet, wear a top, and possibly leg warmers, for the warm-up, then hand them to a helper.
- If position on the start grid is important — that is, in a criterium on a "tight" circuit, or in a mountain-bike race — aim to end your warm-up in time to get a position at the front. And to avoid the possibility of finding the road blocked

when you get to the line, finish your warm-up in the direction the race is starting, then come back, turn your bike round and slot in at the front.
- Older racers will require a longer time to warm up than younger riders.
- Warm up for longer if the weather is cold, or if the race starts up a hill. The shock of going "into the red" will be greater and you should allow for this.
- Drink from your race bottle during your warm-up if the weather is hot: the more fluid you get in now, the better.

IF YOU'RE JUST STARTING OUT...

Club time trials have few formalities to be observed before you start — sign the sign-on sheet, pay the nominal entry fee and pick up your number. Then it's warm up and ride.

Open time trials are scarcely more formal — you will have been allotted a pre-set start time on the start list, which will be in number order, usually from 1 to the time trial limit of 120. Fastest riders will be allotted the "tens" (i.e. numbers 20, 30 etc.), up to the quickest entrant, who will be off last; those who

are quick, but not quite so quick, will be given a "five".

It's worth remembering that if there are 120 riders on the start list, off at one-minute intervals, and you get a late start, you may be going off up to two hours after the first rider. Always base your intended arrival time on your own start time to avoid hanging around.

Time trial starts are usually very relaxed — the numbers are usually laid out on the verge for the riders to collect before trundling off to the start. It's important to bear in mind that the "headquarters" (often it's just a lay-by) where you collect your number may be some way from the actual start: allow time accordingly.

Mountain-bike races are famous for good-humoured chaos, due to the popularity of the sport, which seems to overwhelm many organizers outside the major series. Prepare for the possibility of long queues, and, at big events, a little distance between car parks and the place where you register and collect race numbers: allow lots of time for this. Allow extra time on your journey for bad sign-posting.

Finishing touches: a pro team masseur slaps on the oil before a race in Spain

13:
TROUBLESHOOTING

HEADS, SHOULDERS, KNEES AND TOES, EYES AND EARS AND MOUTH AND NOSE... RACING AND TRAINING CAN TAKE THEIR TOLL OF YOUR BODY. A WHOLE RANGE OF MINOR AILMENTS AND INJURIES ARE WAITING TO CREEP UP AND TAKE YOU UNAWARES. IF YOU WANT TO KNOW THE WARNING SIGNS, AND HOW TO WARD THE GERMS OFF, HERE'S THE SCOOP.

It will come as no surprise to learn that subjecting your body to the added physical stress of training and racing can lead to illness and injury. This chapter aims to do two things. First — since prevention is better than cure — it should provide you with the information needed to avoid some problems common to cyclists. Clearly no one is able to avoid absolutely everything, so secondly it will tell you how best to treat problems that you may encounter.

The body of a racing cyclist is the equivalent of a Formula One racing car, which requires a much greater level of care, fine-tuning and maintenance than the family saloon. The analogy with the cyclist's body will be obvious — if you want your body to perform at peak level, you must look after it in a similar way. Poor self-care is likely to lead to little more than underperformance, failure and disappointment.

For reasons of space, this chapter can only offer basic advice, which it is to be hoped will enable you to avoid problems common in cyclists and deal with others without professional assistance. Clearly, you can't expect to look after everything that goes wrong by yourself, and when you're getting nowhere on your own be prepared to seek expert advice.

In many ways, cycling — on- or off-road — is the ideal way of gaining and maintaining fitness on a lifelong basis. For the most part it entails aerobic endurance efforts that are beneficial to the heart, lungs and muscles. Unlike running or jogging, your ankles, knees, hips and spine are protected from the damaging effects of repetitively pounding your feet on pavement. As with swimming, people who are significantly overweight can get started with relative ease and minimum harm.

Regular exercise of this type not only keeps obesity at bay and reduces the risk of heart disease and strokes, it can also slow down the rate of physical deterioration that occurs with ageing. There is also strong evidence that exercise reduces the risk of mental disease and can even help the general condition of people suffering from anxiety or depression.

There is a negative side — mainly for the older cyclist returning to the sport. There are those who, because of existing disease or a prolonged layoff, should be cautious about how strenuous their activity is. Heart disease may be silent and revealed by injudicious exercise. Accidents are a risk — as pointed out in the section on hard-shell helmets in Chapter 2 — Equipment.

Other topics that have been brought up by the medical and sporting press include a degree of immunosuppression — a reduction in the effectiveness of the body's defensive immune system resulting from overtraining, which can lead to repeated viral infection — and an increased risk of osteoporosis in later life for young women athletes.

CHECK-UPS

Before the start of the Tour de France all riders now undergo a comprehensive medical examination, and although there are wide variations between different countries it is routine for all professionals and many amateurs to undergo some sort of screening medical examination at regular intervals. British Cycling have been doing this kind of check-up on their elite national squad riders for at least 15 years, so it is safe to conclude that if everyone is doing it there must be good reason.

If you can afford it, it is a good idea to get a simple medical check-up in the winter months. You can take along any existing medical problems when you are not competing and get them sorted out before training begins in earnest. If you know that you have a problem that will require investigating, don't waste the winter months and wait until April to consult a doctor or a physiotherapist to get it checked out.

The medical may be no more than a simple history and physical examination followed by a blood test for haemoglobin level, but the sky is the limit as far as athletic medicals go. You can now pay to undergo a highly sophisticated assessment by experienced sports doctors at various places in the UK, but for the majority of competitors this must rate as an unnecessary luxury. Where medicals are concerned, two groups of cyclists are worthy of comment.

YOUNG CYCLISTS

Without wishing to cause undue alarm, it should be pointed out that recent evidence indicates that a small percentage of apparently healthy young people are at a significantly increased risk of sudden death through heart failure during exercise due to a condition called cardiomyopathy.

Experts within the sport's governing bodies are examining this condition closely, and a survey is underway in northern Europe to determine whether training for cycle racing has any effect on increasing the incidence of this condition, which it must be stressed is not common.

Expert examination and special tests are required to diagnose cardio-myopathy, and there are no simple foolproof questions to reveal the people at greatest risk. The most important piece of advice is that any young cyclist who comes from a family where a relative has died suddenly from heart disease before the age of 40 should be checked out for the condition by a specialist.

Retrospectively, some of those who have died from cardiomyopathy can be seen to have had previous warnings that all was not normal. Among these are greater shortness of breath than you would expect for the exercise you are doing, chest pain or palpitations during exercise, and, in particular, collapse during or after exercise.

THE OLDER CYCLIST

It is difficult to lay down the law on who should get a check-up. In an ideal world, everyone over the age of 40 embarking on — or in many cases returning to — the sport should make sure that their physical condition allows them to participate safely.

Certain guidelines are universal: anyone on long-term medication or suffering from heart disease, raised blood pressure, lung disease, arthritis, diabetes or epilepsy should obtain advice from their GP or specialist to discuss the risks and benefits of racing. In general specialists will be all in favour of physical ability and guidance should be sought on the level and intensity of riding and racing that is advisable.

If you are applying to BC for a racing licence, you are obliged to complete a declaration that you are not suffering from any condition that would affect your ability to compete safely. The aim is to protect all competitors from themselves — and to protect those they compete against!

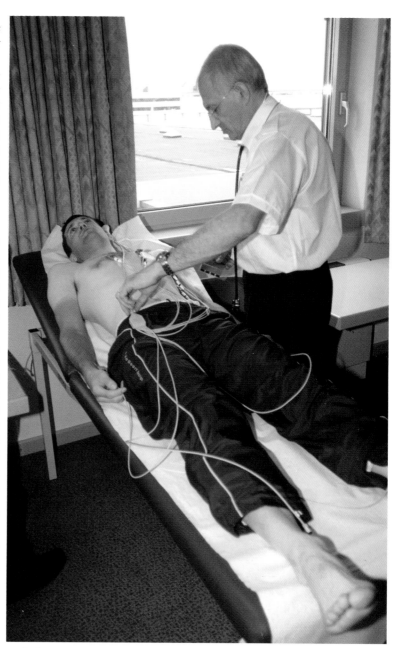

Medical monitoring for pros: you'll have to find your own doctor, but it's worth the effort

COMMON PROBLEMS AND SELF-HELP

COLDS AND FLU

Cycling involves a lot of heavy breathing of cold and damp air, so minor respiratory inflammation and infections are common. However, many people confuse colds and flu, and it is important to know the difference between the two as training with a cold is unlikely to lead to major problems, while training with flu can in some rare cases be dangerous.

Principal cold symptoms are a runny or blocked nose, sore eyes and frequent sneezing, while the temperature isn't usually raised. You can treat yourself simply with decongestant nose drops and/or inhalations of Olbas oil, Friars balsam or similar. If you are going to compete while suffering, be careful not to take any of the cold cures on the market that contain banned substances — they are a regular cause of "accidental" positive drug tests. If in the slightest doubt, don't take it.

Colds and flu are both caused by viruses, but flu is a far more aggressive illness. The symptoms of flu include those of the common cold, but with additional aches and pains in the muscles and joints, shivering, headache, general weakness and a raised temperature. You may be able to "work through" a cold, but you certainly should not attempt to train if you have flu or think you may have.

At the very best, you will simply aggravate the condition and delay your recovery, while in a percentage of flu cases myocarditis (inflammation of the heart muscle) may occur, and if you carry out heavy exercise with this condition abnormal heart rhythms and even death can result. The moral is simple — don't train or race if you have flu.

Wait until muscle aches have gone, your temperature is back to normal, and your resting heart rate is within five beats of its usual morning rate.

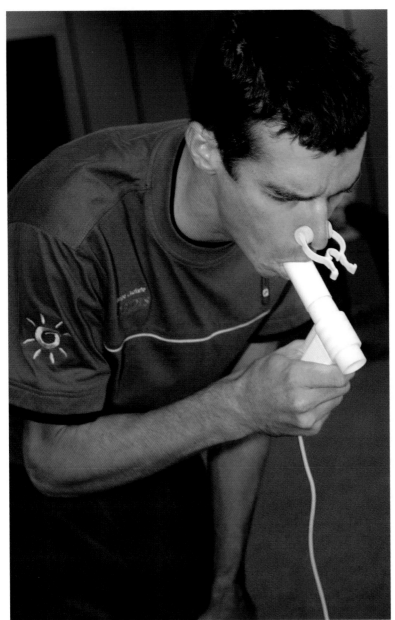

Clearing the tubes: bronchitis is an occupational hazard in cycling

Miguel Indurain winning the 1993 Tour de France while taking antibiotics for an infected tooth.

What does interfere with performance in a big way is the underlying infection for which the antibiotic has been prescribed. They may not be appropriate for every trivial infection — most things will eventually get better without them. In the end it comes down to deciding whether you have the time and patience to let nature do its work.

OTHER COMMON ILLNESSES

GLANDULAR FEVER

Often known as GF or Infectious Mononucleosis ("Mono" in the US), and, more attractively, as "kissing disease". It is very common among people in their twenties, and, surprisingly, many have the infection at what is known as "sub-clinical" level — where there are no major symptoms.

Typically, however, symptoms are an acute sore throat with fever, sweating, and enlargement of the glands in the neck and sometimes the abdomen. Usually, after a relatively short acute illness — often mistaken for tonsillitis, but which isn't cured by antibiotics — there ensues general fatigue and malaise that can continue for weeks or months.

Blood tests will confirm the diagnosis, and some more sophisticated tests can give your doctor an idea of how far the disease has progressed, and how long it will take you to recover. Usually doctors advise that contact sports are stopped for several months to avoid the risk of damaging the spleen, while alcohol is best avoided due to the risk of liver inflammation.

As far as cyclists are concerned, the biggest danger is trying to resume training much too soon. If you do so, the result will be that you impede your recovery and end up being ill for far longer. The motto "when the going gets tough the tough get going" is a good one for racing cyclists, but not where viral infections such as glandular fever are concerned. If you adopt this policy, you will be your own worst enemy.

ASTHMA

An illness that appears to have dramatically increased in incidence over

BRONCHITIS

Very common among cyclists, which is hardly surprising, as serious cyclists ride in all weathers in a climate best described as changeable, inhaling huge amounts of air and traffic fumes, while the temperature and their level of effort can fluctuate dramatically during a long ride.

Bronchitis is usually the result of a cold "going on to the chest", and what started as a simple cold can progress to a dry cough with discomfort behind the breastbone when you breathe deeply. If it goes no further than this, inhalations and a simple cough preparation such as Pholcodine may be all that is needed.

If you reach the point where you're coughing up thick yellow or green phlegm, you should see a doctor and consider whether a course of antibiotics is necessary. You'll almost certainly get better without an antibiotic, but it may take longer, and you will not want to stop training longer than is necessary.

ANTIBIOTICS

There's a myth that taking antibiotics seriously interferes with training and racing, not a view held by most doctors. There is not a great deal of research around the question, but what there is does suggest that antibiotics do not interfere with athletic performance. There is also anecdotal evidence, such as recent years. A large number of elite cyclists, up to world championship and Olympic gold medal standard, are sufferers, and the good news is that most of those affected can control their symptoms with treatment.

There are two main types of asthma that frequently cohabit: sufferers from both kinds experience intermittent attacks of wheezy breathing, varying in severity.

Exercise-induced asthma typically occurs in coolish weather when a major effort is made. It is probably due to the inhalation of too large an amount of cold air for the lungs to cope with. Cold air makes the airways go into spasm, hence the wheezing.

The time triallist who races at the crack of dawn is at high risk. As you continue to ride and the body's core temperature rises — as perhaps does the external air temperature — the problem abates and most cyclists find they can "ride through" the spasm without treatment.

Allergic asthma can occur at any time and can be induced by a variety of factors, including emotion, infection, and allergy to air-borne pollutants and pollens. The main symptom is wheezing, which is generally more severe than that with exercise-induced asthma, and can on occasion be life-threatening.

Both conditions require professional medical help, and treatment usually consists of use of an inhaler. The most commonly used type is Ventolin (Salbutamol), although inhaled steroids such as Becotide are also effective, and sometimes the anti-allergic product Intal may be prescribed.

If you believe you are suffering from asthma, seek help from your GP and do not try to treat it yourself. Make sure that the treatment prescribed is allowable under dope control regulations if you are competing.

It should be noted that all competitors who use asthma inhalers now require a doctor's certificate confirming their diagnosis of asthma and the medical need for this treatment. You are also required to notify British Cycling, who maintain a register of approved users. It is wise to keep a photocopy of the original medical certificate with your racing licence. For further information, check the website for your governing body.

HAY FEVER
Another condition that has increased enormously as a problem for cyclists over the last few years. The reason may in part be the increase in atmospheric pollution from exhaust fumes and so on. It is said that the number of people affected doubles every year. Typically the affected person suffers for a few months every year, and those months are invariably the summer racing season.

The symptoms are repeated sneezing, sore eyes, a blocked or runny nose and sore throat. This does not sound too dramatic, but they can be very severe and are unpredictable. You may get up in the morning in your home town with no symptoms, drive 50 miles to a race and find you have major problems with your hay fever.

This means treatment generally has to be preventative and may consist of antihistamines by mouth or locally active steroid sprays to the nose. Two small points — beware of the older brands of antihistamine tablets: although cheap and effective and available without prescription they can cause severe drowsiness, which will affect your performance. If possible opt for one of the newer, non-sedating medicines rather than the older types such as Piriton.

Secondly, some of the over-the-counter preparations contain substances banned under dope control regulations. As a competing cyclist you should buy all medicines only at a chemist's shop and on the advice of a pharmacist, who can confirm that the medicine is legal for use in competition.

POINTS OF CONTACT
When you get down to serious regular riding your body will take some time to adjust. There are three contact points with your machine where temporary discomfort is likely to arise — firstly, and not surprisingly, the saddle, then the bars and pedals.

THE SADDLE
Over the years there have been a number of myths about how best to acclimatize the backside to the saddle. Fortunately, saddle design has improved dramatically over the last 25 years. There was once a genuine need to "break in" a saddle, which amounted to nothing less than

suffering a degree of ongoing discomfort for some months while the old-style leather saddle became painfully and laboriously moulded to its owner's shape. Now, thanks to new technology, any discomfort is likely to be short lived, but you can still make life easier for yourself in several ways:

- Always wear a pair of genuine cycle shorts, the type with chamois or mock chamois insert. Some new cyclists develop problems because they have bought what they think is the correct garment, but are in fact high-street "fashion" Lycra "cycling shorts".
- Be scrupulous about hygiene in the perineal region — the area of the crutch that is in contact with the saddle.
- Wear shorts only once before washing. This means you will need two pairs at least.
- Use of "chamois cream", available in good bike shops, on the insert is advisable as it will reduce friction.
- Applying alcohol or spirit to the perineal skin to "harden it up" used to be advised. DON'T do it. This will cause cracking of the skin and make you more likely to get an infection.
- If you get redness, develop a cyst or get an infection in this region — see your doctor. He will probably prescribe an antibiotic by mouth or cream that can be put on the area.

THE HANDS
A less obvious area to watch, but prolonged pressure on the hands of novice cyclists can lead to pressure on the nerves supplying the fingertips. The result is numbness in the hands and fingertips, worse when you are riding, and liable to persist for a short time after you get off the bike.

- Get a knowledgeable rider or coach to check your position on the bike to make sure that you aren't putting too much pressure on the hands.
- Avoid the thin type of handlebar tape — use the padded type, two layers if necessary. In extremis, place a layer of foam rubber cushioning under the tape.
- Wear cycling mitts with padded palms to absorb some of the vibration transmitted from the road. They will also protect the palms of your hands if you crash.

THE FEET

The most important interface between you and the bike, transmitting all the energy from your legs to the pedals.

To avoid developing foot or knee problems, novices should follow these rules when buying clipless pedals, as described in Chapter 2:

- Ask specifically for a pedal that allows the front of the foot to rotate slightly.
- Ask the shop to fit the special shoe-plate to your shoes. It's worth paying for the job to be done properly.
- If they don't understand the first question, and are unable to carry out the second task, go and find a shop where they can do both these things.

SOFT TISSUE INJURIES

No matter how careful you are sooner or later you will take a tumble, ending up with superficial skin abrasions from contact with the road — what cyclists describe as "road rash". This isn't a detailed manual on how to deal with all eventualities, but a guide on simple self-treatment of abrasions.

It is essential that all cyclists keep up to date with tetanus immunization. The smallest of cuts and grazes can result in infection with tetanus and sadly several people die, unnecessarily, in the UK from tetanus every year. After a basic course of three injections you only need a booster every 10 years, so it doesn't require much effort.

"Road rash" treatment can be remembered best by the acronym "RICE", which stands for the four main components of treatment:

R — Rest: don't use the damaged part.
I — Ice: applied immediately and indirectly can reduce swelling.*
C — Compression: with a bandage to prevent further swelling.
E — Elevation: keep the affected part raised to reduce swelling.

*Note — Ice applied directly to a wound can produce a burn. Apply intermittently — 5 to 10 seconds every 30 seconds — and

The eyes have it: winter cyclo-cross, and mountain bike racing and road racing in the wet and cold are particularly demanding on the body

wrap it up in a towel in a plastic bag. A packet of frozen peas is excellent and moulds neatly to the shape of the part to which it is applied. Remember not to eat them afterwards!

To this can be added the use of an anti-inflammatory such as Ibuprofen (Brufen in the UK) or Voltarol. Occasionally these can be useful in a cream form applied directly to injured areas.

Points to remember when treating wounds:

- Remove all grit, dirt and grass from wounds. They can act as a focus for future infection.

- If you can't manage this, go to a casualty department where they can.
- Use antiseptic solution (e.g. Savlon or Chlorhexidine) to clean the wound.
- Avoid putting iodine-containing compounds into the wound.
- Expose wounds to the air wherever possible.
- Don't swathe wounds in bandages — less is usually better than more.
- Keep wounds dry. If you can't then bandages are OK.
- Arnica cream is a useful homeopathic remedy for reducing swelling and bruising.
- Take a simple painkiller such as Paracetamol and keep the part gently exercised.

BACKACHE

Cyclists are no more prone to backache than anyone else. The evidence suggests that they are less at risk of developing back problems than competitors in other sports in general and contact sports such as rugby in particular.

This is mainly to do with the non-weight-bearing nature of riding a bike compared with, say, running, and the lack of direct blows other than accidental ones. One study showed that 50 per cent of professional cyclists had suffered from significant backache during their careers, but only 25 per cent had been forced to stop competing for more than two weeks during their careers.

There are two occasions when unusual strain is placed upon cyclists' backs. Firstly, during prolonged efforts in the aerodynamic position on the dropped part of the handlebars in a time trial or road-race break. This can preclude the usual slight changes in position that continually ease the back.

Secondly, in carrying out prolonged climbing "out of the saddle", repetitive minor rotatory forces can be placed on the spine. It is beyond the scope of this book to do more than scratch the surface on this subject, but I'll try to summarize a few points.

- The presence of backache is not necessarily related to your cycling. You may suffer from a pre-existing mechanical back problem that has been revealed or — occasionally — made worse by cycling.
- It is worthwhile getting an experienced coach to take a look at your position on the bike. Experienced coaches say that occasionally they see amateur riders of international level with a totally inappropriate set-up on the bike.
- If your position is correct or if changing it makes no difference, you have a choice of courses of action:
- You can continue with self-help by beginning a course of back-strengthening exercises combined with regular and progressive stretching for the back muscles.
- Or you can consult a doctor, sports-experienced physiotherapist, osteopath

A mechanic tightens a shoeplate on the move: check yours regularly for wear and tear

which may entail x-rays or looking inside the joint with a small device known as an arthroscope. To keep things relatively simple, here is a list of points to consider, which may relate to your knee problem.

- Is your position on the bike correct? This is critical. If you're on a frame that is the wrong size, with the legs over-stretched or compressed due to incorrect saddle height or crank length, after several thousand pedal revolutions your body will stop running smoothly and will send you messages to that effect.
- Are your feet correctly aligned in terms of shoe-plate fittings? If one foot is "toeing in" you will eventually have problems.
- Is there any significant wear in pedals or cranks? Could they have been damaged by a crash, causing minor misalignment?
- Have you had any recent crash or fall that could have resulted in a minor internal injury to the knees?
- Are you keeping your knees warm enough when the weather is cold? There seems to be an increased number of knee injuries in cyclists in spring at about Easter time. Think about keeping your knees covered up or applying a heat rub if you're going to expose them.
- Are you pedalling or pushing? Attempts to "windmill" huge gears are a common cause of knee pain in novice cyclists. This imposes huge pressure on the knee and can lead to tendinitis. The moral is simple — elite cyclists can all pedal smoothly and rapidly, so reduce the gears you are using and learn to spin. It is also more cost-effective in terms of energy.
- Finally — is your training schedule appropriate? Have you recently stepped up your mileage or a specific area of training, which has led to the problem?

The only way to sort out a knee problem is to consult an expert, but hopefully the above will point you in the right general direction, for prevention as well as cure. If you need a little self-treatment (for example, for slight pain in a stage race), start with simple pain killers by mouth,

or chiropractor to determine whether there is an underlying mechanical problem in your back.

- If your symptoms are accompanied by pain or numbness that spreads from the low back into the legs and feet, consult a professional at an early stage.
- Persistent numbness in the saddle contact area or difficulty with bladder control are grounds for an urgent visit to a doctor.

Simple pain killers such as Paracetamol or Ibuprofen are appropriate — they are unlikely to mask the pain totally and can keep you riding. They can be combined with the application of rubbing creams such as Ralgex, Deep Heat or Algipan to the area. They will produce local skin reddening and irritation, which increases the blood supply.

KNEE PROBLEMS

A major cause of worry to cyclists everywhere, but less common as a cause of ongoing disability than you might expect. Like everyone else, cyclists may have underlying mechanical abnormalities of the knee that are exacerbated by the demands of the sport and in particular the repeated up and down action of rapid pedalling. However, mostly the knee acts as a simple hinge joint and doesn't have to cope with the stresses involved in, for example, football.

Diagnosing severe knee problems is a job for an experienced sports doctor, such as Paracetamol, while applying Ibuprofen-type anti-inflammatory creams to the knee itself. However, if simple pain killers aren't effective, it means that you are not fit to race and need to seek medical advice.

HELMETS AND HEAD PROTECTION

If you are new to cycling, you will probably take the idea of head protection for granted, but this has not always been the case, so anyone who needs convincing should bear the following in mind.

No one can claim that helmets either prevent accidents or prevent head injuries. Accidents can only be reduced by personal vigilance and avoidance of risks, but even the most careful cyclist is at the mercy of less careful road users. In a major accident where high speed or direct impact to the head is involved, little will protect the cyclist.

What can be said, however, is that the level of injury will be downgraded. An accident that might have produced concussion may result in no symptoms at all, while one potentially leading to a prolonged period of concussion or worse might end up as no more than a bad headache.

Design of hard helmets is improving all the time — even professional cyclists in

the Tour de France find them acceptable for prolonged racing in extreme heat. They are based on the principle that the polystyrene used in their construction will crumple and deform on an impact, absorbing energy and mopping up the force that might otherwise act directly on the brain.

Ignore the old-style rubber or leather strip helmets sometimes known as "hairnets". You will still see the odd cyclist wearing them (and the term "odd" has been carefully chosen) but these helmets should be consigned to the history books — all they do is prevent some superficial cuts, while not absorbing major impact.

Look for the following in the ideal helmet:

- A hard outer shell (a net-type cover over a polystyrene shell means the shell receives less protection in day-to-day use).
- Thick internal polystyrene liner.
- Straps that adjust widely and easily.
- Design that does not impede vision or hearing.
- Light weight — you should barely notice you have got it on.
- Availability in a variety of sizes.
- Internal pads for precise adjustment to your fit.
- Vents to cool the head in hot weather.

Soft tissue injuries are a regular occurrence but are easily treated: those shorts will take a little more sorting out...

If you do have a spill in a helmet and it is damaged, get a new one. Once the polystyrene has been deformed it won't absorb impact so well in a future crash. When you buy a helmet, try to get one from a manufacturer who will provide you with a free or cheap replacement in case of damage through accident.

WOMEN AND CYCLING

Over the last 30 years, many deeply cherished beliefs about women's sporting abilities have been demolished. It is not that many years ago that the RTTC 12-hour time trial competition record was held by the late Beryl Burton, who did more to destroy the illusion that women cyclists are restricted by physical limitations than anyone else. Sports doctors are persistently asked about three topics by women cyclists: the risk of osteoporosis in later life, dealing with hormonal variations and racing, and cycling in early pregnancy.

OSTEOPOROSIS

All women taking part in endurance sports, together with ballet dancers, tend to have low body fat and low Body Mass Indices on measurement — figures of 19 or 20 or lower for this measure of the density of the body, which gives an indication of obesity or the reverse, are common. Recent research shows that when body fat is low, the menstrual cycle can cease for months or years. Where there is prolonged cessation of periods, oestrogen levels are low, and the density of the bones is often reduced.

In the past it was said that exercise was universally positive, but not in this respect. If bones are not allowed to achieve their optimum density during early adult life (in teens and twenties), they are ill prepared for the thinning that occurs after the menopause. There is thus a major risk that bones will break spontaneously not in the 70s and 80s, but up to 20 years earlier. If periods are slight or absent in a young female cyclist, then taking the contraceptive pill is an effective way of maintaining bone strength — with or without supplementing calcium in the diet.

A Swedish rider falls in a world championship, and the helmet takes much of the impact

Nicole Cooke proving that women can be as dynamic, if not more so, than men when they take to two wheels

disruption to training or racing: a doctor should be consulted, and consideration given to treatment with Ponstan, which reduces pain and also menstrual loss. Where the timing of a period clashes with a major event and is liable to prejudice performance or prove totally inconvenient, it can only be deferred by the use of hormones. These are available only on prescription, so a doctor must be consulted.

FERTILITY AND PREGNANCY

There is no evidence of fertility being affected by cycling – unless your body weight is so low as to affect your periods. As pregnancy progresses, hormonal changes produce some laxity in ligaments, so cycling may be slightly less comfortable than usual, but there is no suggestion that contact with the saddle or the physical activity of cycling has any untoward effects.

Opinions vary about competing during pregnancy, but the consensus is "Don't take part in a sport where you are at risk of a fall that could cause injury to you and the developing baby." Another consideration is that the high demands of exercise may reduce blood flow to the placenta, and exercise at high altitudes is also inadvisable. The question of the body's heat regulation in pregnancy is also complex, and on balance most sports doctors would advise against competition or serious training during pregnancy. It is, however, perfectly safe to remain physically active and ride a bike in pregnancy for as long as is physically comfortable.

OVERTRAINING

"Immunosuppression", or the possibility of heavy training and racing suppressing the body's infection defence systems, is a popular topic of conversation among elite athletes. While it has been shown that moderate physical training – the level that the bulk of competitors are involved with – reduces the risks of infection, prolonged heavy training schedules or intense competition do seem to reduce the content in the blood of the white blood cells that help fight off illness.

As emphasized in Chapter 3, training is a progressive overload of the body's systems, with the aim of producing ever

PERIOD PROBLEMS

Women have become world champions and produced world records at all stages of the menstrual cycle, so it is not really possible to talk of "a favourable time of the month" for competition. The optimum time does seem to remain constant for any one woman – some women will describe their pre-menstrual phase as being best, for others it is the worst.

Women who suffer from heavy or painful periods find this the most major greater workloads — essentially a destructive process. Training regimes must recognize this fact: the periods of rest within a training schedule are as important as time actually spent in training.

The symptoms of overtraining are insidious, and may include loss of enthusiasm, a continual increase in fatigue, irritability, difficulty in relaxing, poor concentration and ever-decreasing performance. You may think it is all due to too little training and make matters worse by increasing the amount you are doing. The message is simple — if things aren't going right, and you feel unhealthy, think about overtraining as a possible cause.

DRUGS IN SPORT

The rules governing drug misuse by athletes are designed to prevent medication being taken to enhance performance — the rules are not trying to prevent athletes from taking medication that they genuinely require for treatment.

Unfortunately, some compounds that are commonly prescribed by doctors can lead to enhanced sporting performance, and their use is thus banned in competition for everyone. Doctors can always prescribe an allowable medicine, so those with a problem don't have to suffer in silence.

Additionally, many medicines available without prescription over the counter in a pharmacy contain banned substances, and many positive drug tests have been innocent and accidental because of this. It is thus essential for all racing cyclists to be aware of the drug regulations and the reasons behind them. Drug tests are not limited to professional racing: they are carried out on a random basis at amateur events in Britain as well.

Drug misuse is a complicated subject that there is not enough space here to explore thoroughly. However, it is sufficient to remind readers that cyclists have died in the past during competition, and the risks are not confined to the short term: if anything, the longer term risks are of even greater concern.

You should also be aware that some "nutritional supplements" have been shown to contain traces of banned substances. This may not be detailed on the packaging and for this reason extreme caution must be taken when purchasing these types of sports supplements. If in any doubt, don't purchase without seeking advice.

The Sports Council has produced several leaflets on the risks of drug misuse in sport, and a video showing the actual drug control procedures carried out in their affiliated sports. A list of banned medications also appears in the *BC Directory*, but I would advise all competing cyclists to contact UK Sport and obtain a copy of their information leaflet. It is credit-card sized, and can be kept with you, so that if you see a doctor or buy medicine at a pharmacy, the card can be shown to confirm that your treatment is "sport use legal".

UK Sport's website includes a database that can be used to check whether the medicine you have been prescribed is cleared for competition. The address is: **www.uksport.gov.uk/did**. Requests for information can also be emailed to **drug-free@uksport.gov.uk**, while phone requests can be made to their answerphone service on 0800 528 0004.

WHEN, HOW AND WHERE TO SEE WHICH DOCTOR?

Government and society may officially encourage participation in sport, but as most sportspeople find out sooner or later, the arrangements for medical care of injuries leaves much to be desired. At worst, anything resulting from sport is treated as a self-inflicted injury, and the sufferer is told by their doctor that they are too old or too young or doing too much. So where and how do you find someone who will treat that sports injury sympathetically?

This book cannot provide a list of names and addresses, but I can indicate some avenues of inquiry to follow — although if you are really fortunate, your GP will be sympathetic to your needs. Most medical students do some sport, but are squeezed out of personal participation after a few years in practice.

When you choose a doctor to register with you should certainly check out whether they have a sports past — in addition, as a general rule, younger GPs will be more sympathetic than their more senior colleagues. You should also check around the members of your local cycling club — who do they see when they have a

problem? If this produces no result, ask around the local football and rugby clubs — the chances are that they have a local doctor whom they use for their teams, or they will have the name of the nearest sports injury clinic.

There are quite a number of these now around the country, but most run on a private basis, and you will be obliged to pay for the initial consultation and any treatment. There are also a small number of NHS Sports Injury clinics — you will need to be referred to one of them by your GP. If you see the qualifications MSc or Diploma in Sports Medicine after a doctor's name, you're almost certainly in safe and sympathetic hands.

Don't confine yourself to seeking out a doctor for your care. An experienced, sports-orientated qualified physiotherapist will often be of greater value to you where soft-tissue injury is concerned. The same is true of other qualified health professionals such as chiropractors and osteopaths. Get recommendations from the sources above, but confirm that the person you are consulting has a registered qualification and beware of enthusiastic and unqualified amateurs.

If you are a member of BC, you can obtain advice on medical matters by writing to them, and where appropriate your letter will be passed on to the BC medical officer for his suggestions. BC may also be able to provide some assistance in locating an established sports injury clinic or sports doctor in your area.

Other lists of sports doctors and clinics are maintained by the British Olympic Association and the British Association of Sports Medicine. You will not be able to obtain direct access to this information yourself, but your doctor will be able to obtain the names and addresses of specialist doctors and facilities for you.

A doctors' organization called UKADIS (UK Association of Doctors in Sports Medicine) was established a couple of years ago with the purpose of increasing the quality of sports medical care. UKADIS members look after the majority of the elite sportsmen and -women within the UK. Your GP might wish to contact this organization if specialist referral or advice is needed.

14: **STRETCHING**

STRETCHING IS NOT SOMETHING MANY CYCLISTS TAKE SERIOUSLY, BUT IT IS OF VITAL IMPORTANCE IN WARDING OFF INJURY AND MAINTAINING SUPPLENESS IN AREAS WHICH ARE NOT EXERCISED ON THE BIKE. MUSCLES TRAINED FOR STRENGTH TEND TO SHORTEN, WITH A REDUCED SPAN OF MOVEMENT AND CONSEQUENT INCREASED RISK OF INJURY.

If you are more supple, you are less likely to develop the knee, back and shoulder injuries which, at best, stop you training for a short time, and, at worst, ruin your cycling altogether. You are also less likely to injure yourself if you crash.

The following programme of stretches should help maintain basic suppleness around the body. However, it is important to bear in mind the following points:

- Do not stretch until you feel pain. Stretch until you can feel the stretch, and hold for between 10 and 30 seconds.
- Don't give up stretching at the end of the season. Stretch all year round, even if you are not riding that day.
- If injured, keep stretching, except in the injured area. Otherwise you will lose flexibility in other areas of your body which may cause problems when you return to training.
- Stretch before and after exercise sessions. You should not stretch from cold, however, as the muscles are less supple if they have not been warmed up by a little light exercise.
- Don't rush. Stretching should relax you. If you try to stretch quickly, you risk injury.

1–3 SHOULDERS AND SIDE

Hold hands in front of the body, palms away from you. Gradually stretch as far forwards as you can, then as high above the head as you can.

4 FRONT OF SHOULDERS

Clasp your hands behind the body, then move them up and back as far as you can, with the back held straight and the head looking forwards.

5 SHOULDER AND SIDES

Clasp one elbow behind the head, then pull gently across behind the back of the head. Repeat for the other arm.

6–7 SIDES

With the knees bent a little, extend one arm above the head and lean carefully towards the opposite side, being careful to keep the back straight. Repeat with the other arm.

8–9 LOWER BACK

Lying on your back, which should remain flat, move both knees to the chest, hold with the hands, and raise the head to the knees.

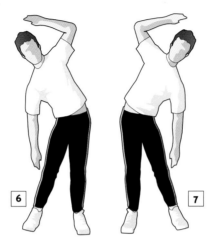

157

10 FRONT OF BODY

Lying on your front, move the hands to shoulder level and gently lift the upper body, pushing the head back and keeping the lower body on the floor.

11 LOWER BACK AND HIP

With the knee bent, position the foot on the outside of the other leg. Turn the upper body carefully to the bent knee and push to move the body round a little further. Repeat for the other side.

12–13 BACK OF THIGH

Lying on your back, move the knee towards the chest, hold under the thigh and pull gently, feeling the lower back stretch. Holding the thigh, straighten the leg. Repeat for the other side.

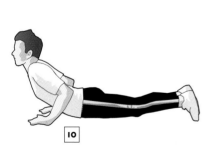

14–15 INNER THIGH, LOWER BACK

Sit with one knee bent, flat on the floor,
with the foot on the inside of the opposite
thigh. Lean gently forwards and stretch
down the straight leg towards the ankle.
Repeat for the other leg.

16 FRONT OF THIGH AND HIP

Use a wall or a table to keep your
balance. Start with the legs together, raise
one knee behind you and hold the ankle.
With the upper body straight, gently pull
the foot towards the buttock. Repeat for
the other leg.

17 CALF

Stand a couple of feet away from a wall,
and lean against it. Move one foot
forwards, then, with the heel down, slowly
move the hips downwards. Repeat for the
other side.

18 BACK OF ANKLE

Lean against a wall with the feet about 18
inches apart. With the heels down, bend
the knees and lean the hips forwards.

19–21 BACK OF LEG

Standing straight, cross the legs and keep
the feet together. Then, with the front
knee slightly bent, bend gently down to
touch the toes. Repeat for the other leg.

INDEX